First Steps to Excellence in College Teaching

Third Edition

by
Glenn Ross Johnson

Atwood Publishing
Madison, WI

First Steps to Excellence in College Teaching
3rd edition
© 1995 by Magna Publications, Inc.
All rights reserved

Atwood Publishing
2710 Atwood Ave.
Madison, WI 53704
608-242-7101

Cover design by Evan Schultz
Edited by Robert Magnan

Library of Congress Cataloging-in-Publication Data

Johnson, Glenn R., 1934-
        First steps to excellence in college teaching / by Glenn Ross Johnson
                p. cm.
Includes bibliographical references.
ISBN 0-912150-42-4
1. College teaching -- United States. 2. First year teachers -- United States. I. Title.
LB2331.j565   1995
378.1'25--dc20   95-17198
                                                                      CIP

Table of Contents

Preface

National reports, books by prominent educators, and legislative mandates continue to call for changes in higher education. Students, parents, taxpayers, public officials, governors, and boards of regents are screaming for reform. The more conservative and objective criticisms express a sense of urgency, a plea to systematically analyze the situation within each department and/or college and to take appropriate action to better prepare beginning instructors and reward excellent teachers. The bottom line is clear: there is a crisis involving college and university teaching in the United States.

Widespread media attention has focused on the quality of instruction in colleges and universities. Robert J. Braun, Education Editor for the *Newark* (NJ) *Sunday Star-Ledger*, succinctly summarized the situation in an editorial:

> Ironically, teaching — the art or science of pedagogy — is not even considered a worthy object of study among college faculty. ... College teachers, or at least most of them, do not learn how to teach; they study their discipline and then are afflicted on undergraduates with the assumption that knowledge of subject matter will cover a multitude of sins involving a lack of knowledge about the presentation of that subject matter.

Braun continued his attack with the following comments:

> Teaching has never really counted for much in higher education or in the careers of those who work in higher education. Students appreciate good teachers, but institutions have not. When college faculty members present themselves for reappointment, promotion, or

tenure, what is evaluated are indicators of scholarship, not pedagogy. How extensively a man or woman has published is considered more important than how effectively he or she has taught. The college faculty members who devote their time to improving their instructional presentations have short careers.

Higher education systems have ignored the problem. But they need to be proactive in recognizing the importance of teaching. They need to prepare the professors of tomorrow for teaching.

They can do that through programs designed for graduate teaching assistants, the future professors. They can develop programs to support new teachers, and they can reward great teachers.

They also need to take corrective action with individuals who display a disregard for students and how they learn. Poor instructors need to be confronted. That should take place at the departmental level. Experienced faculty members need to provide advice and support. The department chair needs to establish formal conferences with beginning instructors and teaching assistants if they need to improve their teaching skills.

Staff members in instructional development centers do not, and should not, have the authority to correct poor teaching situations; determining intervention is not their role. The logical step is for administrators to counsel individuals into seeking the services of personnel in instructional development centers.

Instructional development centers can help new faculty and teaching assistants improve their instruction — if the instructors are willing to seek help. Instructional development centers are support and service organizations, available to provide knowledge about the art, science, and research of pedagogy. They can lead instructors to water and perhaps make them so thirsty that they partake in the wealth of instructional strategies. But they can't do the teaching for the instructors. Teachers do the teaching — and many do it very, very well.

Because of the widespread attention given to the poor quality of instruction in colleges and universities, I have turned to another way to help beginning instructors and teaching assistants — by writing this book. Faculty members, teaching assistants, and prospective instructors who read the book will find the suggestions tempting. They will build their knowledge in pedagogy. They will be able to match their personalities with instructional strategies that might improve their teaching.

You may want to skim this entire book, then return to specific chapters at appropriate times. If you are a beginner, you may want to seek advice from experienced instructors with reputations as outstanding teachers. They can help you with those areas in which you may be weak. Once you identify areas where you lack information, you could look at this book's table of contents and decide which chapter to read first, which to read second, and so forth, skipping those areas in which you believe you have real strengths.

Determining
Your Objectives

C ourse objectives should consist of explicit statements about the ways in which students are expected to change as a result of your teaching and the course activities. These should include changes in thinking skills, feelings, and actions.

Most instructors tend to state objectives in such broad terms that students have difficulty interpreting them, and instructors would probably have an equally hard time measuring the progress of the students in achieving the objectives. Several studies have revealed significant increases in learning when students receive a set of behavioral objectives prior to instruction.

Specificity

Instructors usually need to be more explicit in describing their objectives. How do you write explicit objectives? The key is *specificity*.

Consider this objective: "The student will know the history of the United States." What is the meaning of the objective? How would you build a course to meet this objective?

The objective is too broad and may be interpreted in many different ways. This lack of clarity and specificity doesn't help you in planning to teach your course. How would you evaluate the success of the students? What types of evaluation tools would you use to determine if the students have achieved the objective? The objective simply isn't explicit enough to use.

Consider this objective: "The student will understand the reasons for the Civil War." There would be great disagreement among faculty if you asked them to measure the success of the students based on this objective.

Objectives should communicate *exactly* what you want the students to accomplish. Objectives stated specifically are more useful than general aims. Broad goals and broad objectives may be of value for some programs, but they are not as valuable to you when you attempt to plan your course. Both you and your students need to know where the course is going.

You might begin to plan your course with only a few broad statements about concepts, topics, principles, and/or generalizations for the course. For example, before writing your objectives, you might begin with a statement such as the following: "I want these students to know about the important issues that were being debated in the country just prior to the Civil War." From this broad topic, you can move to specific objectives when planning your individual class sessions.

Behavior

Another important point is that the specific objectives need to reflect *student behavior*. If you think only about your own behavior, you have nothing that reflects the true progress of the students; to assess student progress, you need objectives written in terms of measurable student behavior.

How do you write an objective that reflects student behavior? Answer this question: "What do I want the student to do at the end of this class period that he or she probably can't do when the class begins?" Having answered that question, begin to think in behavioral terms that are more easily measurable.

Read these objectives:

- The student will know the names of the Civil War generals.
- The student will understand the term 'carpetbagger.'
- The student will appreciate the concerns of families during the Civil War.
- The student will enjoy the music of the Civil War era.
- The student will really understand the problems of the South in financing the Civil War.

How can you measure the behavior of the student at the close of the class session or the end of the course if the objective states that the student will "know" or "understand" or "appreciate" or "enjoy"?

Importance

Another consideration is the relative importance of your objectives. If we compare the objectives listed above against the Bloom taxonomy of

Figure 1.1 Bloom's Taxonomy

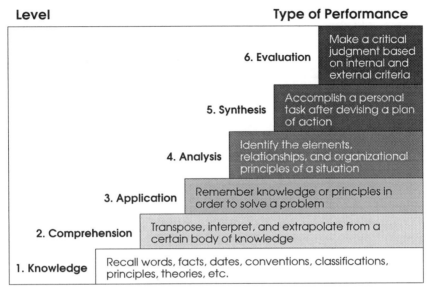

Level   **Type of Performance**

Level	Type of Performance
6. Evaluation	Make a critical judgment based on internal and external criteria
5. Synthesis	Accomplish a personal task after devising a plan of action
4. Analysis	Identify the elements, relationships, and organizational principles of a situation
3. Application	Remember knowledge or principles in order to solve a problem
2. Comprehension	Transpose, interpret, and extrapolate from a certain body of knowledge
1. Knowledge	Recall words, facts, dates, conventions, classifications, principles, theories, etc.

Adapted from B. S. Bloom, et al., 1956.

educational objectives (Figure 1.1), we notice that some of the objectives are more important. History instructors would no doubt agree, for example, that understanding the situation of the South in financing the Civil War involves a more sophisticated level of cognition than knowing the names of the Civil War generals.

This aspect of cognitive level is especially significant if we want our students to do more than just retain facts — if we want them to understand, to apply what they learn, and to think critically.

Clarity of terminology

You should not use words that are open to many different interpretations. Specific objectives use clear words that make it easier to measure behaviors.

Consider this objective: "During a short essay test, the student will identify the major contribution made by each of three generals for the North during the Civil War, and the student will support the contribution with at least one documented piece of evidence for each."

Note that this objective is specific, and even includes the type of examination to be used.

Sometimes, it is advisable to include an acceptable performance level as part of the objective. If only a few students are reaching the minimum acceptable performance level, it is feedback to you that something may be wrong with the instruction. If large numbers of students are reaching a performance level of 90%, it is feedback to the low-scoring students that they have a gap in their learning, they need to study in more depth, or they may need to seek your counsel. Acceptable performance levels also provide the students with a common reference point by which to judge their behavior.

For example, consider this objective: "During a regularly scheduled weekly track contest, the student will run the 100-meter dash in less than 11 seconds."

We know the conditions under which the behavior will be performed (during a weekly track contest), the type of measurable behavior (run the 100-meter dash), and the acceptable performance level (less than 11 seconds). This is an example of a specific behavioral objective. Without the specified acceptable performance level (less than 11 seconds), even I could achieve the objective of running the 100-meter dash — but I could do it in 30 seconds if there were no acceptable performance level specified.

Appropriateness

Let us return to the Civil War for another type of contrast among objectives. Compare these two objectives:

- The student will appreciate the problems confronting the South during the Civil War.
- The student will list 10 generals who fought in the Civil War.

Which of the two objectives is more appropriate for a course in history? The first objective is more appropriate, even though it is not written in specific measurable terms. The second objective is written in specific measurable terms, but it does not require much thinking. Merely stating an objective in specific behavioral terms does not make the objective valuable.

Domains

We usually teach to three major domains:

- Cognitive: knowledge and intellectual skills
- Affective: interests, attitudes, values, appreciations, and adjustments

- Psychomotor: manipulative and motor skills

In the preceding section, all of the objectives that referenced the Civil War, except for the one about appreciating the concerns of the families, fall into the cognitive domain. The example about the 100-meter dash was a psychomotor objective.

Of the three types of domains, objectives in the affective area seem most difficult to describe in behavioral terms. This is complicated by the lack of valid testing procedures to measure feelings and emotions. Nonetheless, many scholars consider the affective domain to be very important.

One approach to setting affective objectives is to ask experienced colleagues for their insights. They have watched students march through their programs and enter "the real world." They have had an opportunity to interact with the employers of their graduates and obtain feedback about the behavior of students in "the real world." Ask experienced teachers for advice and their reactions to your affective objectives.

Another approach is to refer to a publication by Bloom, Hastings, and Madaus, *Handbook on Formative and Summative Evaluation of Student Learning* (1971), which has some very interesting comments about affective objectives. The authors believe that the cognitive domain is a building block for affective domain objectives. They believe that the cognitive beginning is the lowest level of an affective hierarchy, since the student is only aware of a phenomenon. At the next level, the student is willing to deal with the phenomenon through an expression of feelings. Next, the student reacts to the phenomenon, conceptualizing behaviors and feelings and organizing them into a structure. Finally, the student reaches the highest level of the affective hierarchy when the structure becomes a part of his or her perspective on life.

Selecting Textbooks and Developing a Syllabus

There are bad texts — which someone else writes —
good texts — which we write — and perfect texts —
which we plan to write someday.

Kenneth Eble,
The Craft of Teaching:
A Guide to Mastering the Professor's Art

Textbooks are common in undergraduate courses, particularly in required courses. They can be viewed as lectures in print if the textbooks have well-organized chapters, have updated content, and are readable. Hollabaugh (1989) focused his attention on the issue of readability, and he provides a "fog index" that he used to compare the readability of five introductory astronomy textbooks. I have included some additional warnings below.

Some textbooks transmit cultural information. The way the author uses words to describe events and people may be slanted in a positive, negative, or neutral way. The author may have excluded some very important cultural events and minority people when presenting information. If the author's prejudices are apparent, even subtle, you may want to search for a more appropriate textbook.

Textbooks reflect the values of the discipline. Within disciplines there are many different groups, and each group may hold some very strong values that may or may not be appropriate for your course. The more diverse the opinions and representations of such groups within the textbook, the better. Mitch (1990) stated that textbooks should adequately capture issues that are complex, present good argumentation, and provide evidence to support conclusions and generalizations.

Textbooks promote intellectual development. How much depth does the textbook reflect? Is the content on a high enough level to challenge the students? Is there evidence of a variety of cognitive levels throughout the textbook and in the questions that the author might raise, (e.g., application, analysis, synthesis, problem-solving)?

Textbooks can communicate specific biases. This probably sounds similar to the first caution about cultural prejudices. However, in using the term "bias" I mean "perspective" or "orientation." There may be different theories or ways of approaching the historical significance of an event, and the author may deliberately exclude one or another from among theories and perspectives. I lean in the direction of giving fair treatment to competing theories and perspectives.

There are other reasons for selecting a textbook carefully. Many students find it difficult to take accurate notes when listening to an hour of uninterrupted lecture. They rely heavily on their textbook to clarify the content as they review their classroom notes. The more closely the textbook corresponds to their notes, the more useful it should be to the students.

Most textbooks do not always parallel your syllabus, unless you've written your own for the course. Some instructors create their own textbooks from scratch or by compiling the most appropriate materials from various sources. Many others shape their syllabus according to a specific textbook. Most instructors, however, find it necessary to supplement the textbook with ancillary materials. You could distribute readings, copies of charts and graphs, and other handouts and/or arrange with copy centers or bookstores to prepare and sell supplementary course materials for you.

Two important points:

- Always obtain permission from the author and publishing company before duplicating copyrighted materials. This is a question of professional ethics, of course, but there are also legal risks that could prove costly.

- Order textbooks and supplemental materials early, so that they are available at the beginning of the term; the best textbook in the world is of little value if it arrives too late or if the supply of copies is insufficient.

In her article "Selecting the Textbook," Delivee L. Wright, Director of the Teaching and Learning Center at the University of Nebraska-Lincoln, asks the following basic questions:

- Will you supplement the content in the textbook? Or will the textbook be used to supplement what you state in the classroom?
- Do you want the textbook to be the main focus of the course? Or is it merely one of several sources that you want the students to use?

Cost

Textbooks cost more than ever, which makes the price of a text an important consideration — even more so than 20 years ago, when Eble (1976) summarized the problem:

> For most courses, there never has been such an abundance of useful text materials. Faculty members who tend to take advantage of these riches may total the costs for an individual course, but fail to consider that students are expected to buy books for four or five courses.

High costs may discourage some students from purchasing and using all of the textbooks selected for a single course. You must take special care in selecting the number of books you will require students to buy, eliminating those rarely referenced in lectures or on examinations.

You may want to consider putting the less important readings on library reserve. If you do so, visit the library and verify that the readings are actually on reserve. Don't assume anything or expect students to tell you if a reading is unavailable.

Using the textbook

You should learn to use a textbook without repeating what is in print. For example, you might use part of a class period to clarify or supplement the material in the textbook, then devote the remainder of the time to discussions or to asking questions involving application, analysis, synthesis, or problem-solving based on the material presented in the textbook.

As Eble (1976) points out, "If ... stimulating learning through interaction between student and teacher is the chief aim, then what the teacher does in class differs in kind and substance from what the text does." Instructors who merely repeat the text are wasting valuable opportunities for real teaching activities, encouraging students not to read, boring students who've prepared, and/or undermining attendance, participation, enthusiasm — and learning.

Brown and Thornton (1971) suggest that the instructor supplement, elaborate, interpret, or clarify ideas that appear in the textbook. Instructors can help students learn how to use the textbook as a study guide by discussing its organization and treatment of topics, by suggesting ways to study it systematically, and by emphasizing the review, graphic, and index materials.

For example, you could become a role model for the students by simulating how you read the first chapter, pointing out that one usually begins with an overview of the chapter by reading the title, by analyzing the opening paragraph and the summary paragraph in the chapter, and by raising questions that were triggered by the overview. You could also contact the publisher to find out if there is an instructor's guide for the book and if there are special materials available, such as graphs, charts, maps, etc.

Why should you use or not use a textbook?

Fuhrmann and Grasha (1983) and Brown and Thornton (1971) provide excellent guidelines for answering this basic question, in terms of advantages and disadvantages:

Advantages
- Textbooks provide students with uniform bodies of basic information.
- Textbooks contain an organized, sequential approach to the study of a subject, in a simple style and at an appropriate reading level.
- Textbooks include pertinent illustrations, graphs, maps, and diagrams.
- Textbooks present a large amount of information efficiently.
- Textbooks are organized in such a way that you could develop the course syllabus in sequence with the chapters in the book.
- Textbooks contribute to motivation if the expert's insights are presented in an exciting and challenging way.
- Textbooks provide opportunities for students to reason and expand their understanding, if the author has inserted key questions throughout the text.
- Textbooks reduce the in-class time needed for integrating content and thus allow for application, analysis, and problem-solving.

Disadvantages

- Textbooks become outdated and do not provide current innovations.

- Instructors may rely on textbooks as the only source for content, instead of using the information in the book to build concepts, illustrations, examples, and theories within the context of their students' background.

- It takes time to select good textbooks.

- Textbooks may become the crutch for determining objectives. You should select textbooks according to your objectives, not let the textbooks determine your objectives.

- Textbooks allow little or no room to select content from original sources and current research reports.

A systematic checklist for selecting textbooks

In "Selecting the Textbook," Wright (1987) offers an excellent checklist as a systematic guide for selecting textbooks. I present this checklist here, with some minor modifications. You may want to reference this checklist the next time you select your textbooks.

Title: _____

Author(s): _____

Publisher and publication date: _____

Use the following scale to assess each criterion:

1 = very adequate
2 = adequate
3 = neither adequate nor inadequate
4 = inadequate
5 = very inadequate

Scale **Criterion**

1 2 3 4 5 **Bibliography**
Are the citations current and appropriate?

1 2 3 4 5 **Author**
Is he or she recognized as knowledgeable in this particular field?

1 2 3 4 5   **Reviews**
Have professional journal reviews been good?

1 2 3 4 5   **Topic emphasis**
Do topics correspond to objectives for your course?

1 2 3 4 5   **Sequence**
Are topics arranged in a desirable sequence? Can they be adapted without disrupting the usefulness of the book?

1 2 3 4 5   **Content**
Is it accurate? Is the point of view consistent with the current thinking in the field? Are recent developments included?

1 2 3 4 5   **Bias**
Is it free of nationalistic, racial, or sexual bias?

1 2 3 4 5   **Concepts, principles, generalizations**
Are they clearly developed? Can you read basic facts and information in the book and find that they lead you to concepts, principles, and generalizations?

1 2 3 4 5   **Details**
Is detail sufficient?

1 2 3 4 5   **Explanations**
Are they clear and succinct?

1 2 3 4 5   **Reading level**
Is the readability level of the text at a level appropriate for the average student enrolling in your course?

1 2 3 4 5   **Presumed student experience**
Do students have sufficient background to understand the author's material?

1 2 3 4 5   **Titles, headings, subheadings**
Do these help the student visualize the organization and relationship of content?

1 2 3 4 5   **Sources**
Are these documented adequately?

1 2 3 4 5 Summaries, review questions

Are there study aids? Do they help students generalize, apply, and evaluate content? Do they stimulate critical thinking or require problem-solving? For example, after presenting some important information, does the author challenge the students with a simulated happening or real problem to solve?

1 2 3 4 5 Table of contents, preface, index, appendices

Are these adequate and useful? For example, does the author provide a succinct outline of the book in the table of contents? Does the author give a good overview in the preface regarding where the book is going and the type of reader he or she is addressing? Is the index complete with key words and important terms? Do the appendices include any important survey instruments or measurement devices referenced in the body of the text?

1 2 3 4 5 Illustrations

Are these accurate, purposeful, properly captioned, and placed near the related text?

1 2 3 4 5 Graphs, tables, maps, charts

Are these clear, pertinent, and carefully done?

1 2 3 4 5 Durability

Is the book well-constructed? Is the binding flexible?

1 2 3 4 5 Type

Is it clear, easily readable, and large enough?

1 2 3 4 5 Format

Do page size, column arrangement, margins, and white spaces contribute to communicating ideas? Do they allow for supplemental notetaking? Does the format invite reading — or does it impede the reader?

1 2 3 4 5 Price

Is the price reasonable for the extent to which you will use the text for assignments?

1 2 3 4 5 Measurements for student achievement

Are test items or other devices for assessment provided?

1 2 3 4 5 **Size and weight**

Will the text be easily carried to class? Remember: students may have to carry several materials for many courses, sometimes for considerable distances.

1 2 3 4 5 **Instructor's manual**

Are supplemental materials, teaching aids, test questions, and suggested strategies included?

1 2 3 4 5 **Supplemental workbook, computer software**

Are resource materials suitable for some or all students to purchase?

Developing a syllabus

The course syllabus should reflect the overall direction of the course and the objectives you have in mind for the students. Colleagues can show you how they taught the course during previous semesters. Most content decisions are up to you, unless there is a required departmental syllabus. Hammons and Shock (1994, p. 7) declare: "Above all else, the syllabus is a means for improving communication between the instructor and the student."

Distribute the syllabus and provide time for the students to read through it. Invite the students to ask questions about the items in the syllabus.

There are several items to incorporate in the syllabus:

Your full name, title, office location, office phone number, and office hours on the first page. You would be surprised at the number of students who are reluctant to ask questions about these items. Draw a diagram on the board so they can better understand the location of your office. Tell them that you adhere to your office hours, and encourage them to take advantage of those hours if they are having problems. Some instructors include their home phone numbers, while others prefer privacy when away from the campus.

The course title, catalog number, credits, location, days, and time. These may seem like mundane items, but many new students get confused about them. Some even attend the wrong course or wrong section of the course for an entire class session before they realize their mistake. Include the above in the syllabus and help save students from such embarrassment.

A short course description and any prerequisites. Be sure they fit with the statements in the catalog. You don't want to find yourself on the carpet with administrators because you decided to arbitrarily change such items — the descriptions and prerequisites probably reflect numerous hours of deliberation by your colleagues. The students have no excuse if later they claim, "I didn't know the course was going to cover that kind of stuff" and "I don't have the background information."

The titles of basic texts. Specify editions. Bookstores have big sales of used books; there may be problems if new students purchase earlier editions. Sometimes the information is outdated. Sometimes, in literature courses, there are problems with various editions of the same work, since they have different critical apparatuses and pagination, making assignments and class references confusing.

A set of general objectives for the course. Don't include your daily lesson objectives. I have found that four or five really important objectives serve a vital purpose in guiding the students. Review the earlier section on objectives before you choose those for your syllabus.

A set of topics and activities for the semester. Include any special dates for examinations and lab exercises, as well as due dates for papers. These are very helpful to the students — and for keeping you on.

The bibliography, library reserve room references, and audio-visual materials, with their locations. Don't be surprised if students ask, "What's a reserve room?" Answer politely, telling where it is located in the library and what the procedures and restrictions are for using materials on reserve. Sometimes students who are unfamiliar with "routine matters" may avoid crucial preparation or supplemental work.

A statement about academic dishonesty from your institution's student handbook, to ensure that there are no misunderstandings. If you are requiring written work, take time during the first class session to explain plagiarism. Discuss some examples of plagiarism.

There are some additional items that you may want to consider including in the syllabus:

- What is your stand on absences? Does your institution have a policy on absences?
- Will you allow a make-up if a student misses an exam? How will you deal with late term papers?
- Do you want to describe your criteria for grading term papers? How will grades be determined?
- Does the institution have a policy on grading? For example, are you required to use a standard curve when grading? What will constitute an A, B, C, D, or F in the course?

Final details

Make arrangements for teaching aids well in advance of the first class meeting. Check the overhead projector, microphone, film projector, or slide projector; ask a technician to show you how to replace bulbs and/or batteries. Find out where you can obtain immediate assistance if the equipment malfunctions. Many an excellent lesson plan falls apart because of equipment problems.

Stand in the spot where you will lecture. Practice with the equipment you'll be using during class. Note how well your voice carries and how your handwriting looks on the blackboard or on the projection screen. Have another person sit in various seats to give you feedback from students' perspectives.

Such details may take a little extra time, but the results will justify your investment. You'll be better prepared — and more confident.

Those First Class Days

H ow important is that first day of class? Crucial! Both students and instructors find the first session to be a time of anxiety. But the first meeting can also be exciting if properly handled. Here are a few ideas to make a good beginning toward an excellent semester.

Introduce yourself to the students, then have the students introduce themselves. Have them mention their fields of study, hometowns, campus residences, hobbies, and families. This icebreaker shows your interest in the students. It also makes it easier for them to form relationships early in the semester so that they can work together, both in class and outside.

Ask the students to identify some problems or issues they hope to cover during the course. List them on the board. Ask questions that will clarify exactly what they are seeking. These short interactions also help to build an accepting climate within the classroom.

Take attendance for at least the first few meetings. Many instructors overlook this dreaded burden, but it can express your interest in the students as individuals, with faces and names. It also confirms that attending class is important.

Distribute the course syllabus and highlight the most important items. Discuss the purpose of the course and your requirements. Review important dates and compare them with the institution's calendar of events — the deadline for course withdrawals without penalty, the date when grades are due, religious holidays, and so forth. Present campus policies on observing religious holidays and your personal policy on giving makeup tests. Inform the students about the process for appealing grades. Tell them about your positions on student collaboration on homework, work turned in late, and grading. Offer some successful learning strategies for studying for your course.

Students may react to your behavior by imitating you when they interact with others. If you are negative and aggressive with students, and if you make sarcastic remarks during the first class session, it is possible that the students will mimic such behavior.

Beware of the effects of negative conditioning. (See classic studies by B.F. Skinner, Ivan P. Pavlov, John Watson, and Edward Thorndike as reported by Wittrock, 1977.) High-anxiety students seem to perform poorly on a task if they are reprimanded throughout its performance. Such students may be conditioned to feel uncomfortable in similar classrooms in future courses because the sarcastic instructor becomes the students' "conditioned stimulus," creating high anxiety and poor work.

In contrast to the above, I believe you should be curious, considerate, kind, imaginative, and flexible, thus providing a more enriching model for students to copy.

Some instructors erroneously assume that students are lazy. Students may be highly motivated to learn if the subject is of value to them, but they may be bored to tears if you use the same illustrations and examples as the textbook.

Instructors can fall victim to another trap if they believe that the students are stupid. The less talented students may start the course with high expectations, but they may be turned off because the instructor uses illustrations that none of the students understand, in the interest of making the course challenging. Use relevant illustrations that are appropriate for the experiential background of the students, to increase their attention span.

Some instructors like to conclude the first class session with an assigned reading. Others require something in writing, to be collected during the next class session. The idea is to communicate to the students from the very beginning that the course is important. Therefore, whatever the assignment might be, make sure it is valuable, not just a "Mickey Mouse" activity.

If a lab or a field experience is involved, review any safety rules and regulations. You may want to demonstrate some of the precautions the students should take throughout the course. If you teach in the evening, you may provide some additional cautions about campus security.

Some instructors give the students a few sample test items or examples of quality term papers from previous semesters. You may at least want to give the students some hints about how to study for your exams.

Some instructors also develop and administer a diagnostic evaluation the first day of class. These diagnostics are not assigned grades; they cover prerequisite knowledge or skills needed to succeed in the course. After checking the responses and analyzing the data, you may want to reorganize the tentative schedule if students already have mastered the information for one or more topics. Sometimes the data indicate a need for a review of prerequisites prior to undertaking a topic. You may even have students who are totally lacking in the prerequisite knowledge or skills, and you may have to counsel them out of your course and into a course that covers the prerequisites.

Beyond the first few days

Greet the students individually as they enter the room each day. This helps to establish rapport, and it provides students another opportunity to comment about the progress of the course.

Start and finish your class on time. If you start on time, the students know that you mean business, and they will try harder to get there for the beginning of class. Closing on time is also important because some students will have other courses or commitments.

Some instructors play music while the students are entering the classroom. When the music stops, it cues the students that class is about to begin.

Relax! Use humor if appropriate. Project a comic on the screen and relate it to the day's content. Students will look forward to seeing the comics when they enter the classroom. Tell a story about yourself, one that shows the human side — a "goof" that you made, something you forgot to do, a special event like a wedding anniversary.

Share something from *The Wall Street Journal*, *The New York Times*, or a prominent city newspaper, or tell them an anecdote during the first few minutes. This provides time for the students to settle in for the day's lesson.

During class, move around the room — without becoming a distraction. This gets you closer to the students, particularly if the section meets in an auditorium. It is also surprising how your closeness to students keeps them from dozing during class time.

At the close of the class session, congratulate the student who asked the best question during the period, and ask the others why the question was the best.

After you get better acquainted with the students, set up a three-member advisory committee to meet with you each week in your office to provide feedback. How are the other students progressing in the course? Are there any problems so far? What have the students found as strengths?

Ask the students if they want to form study groups and support groups. Have them meet and develop a group roster with addresses, telephone numbers, and electronic mail addresses, if they don't consider such to be an invasion of privacy.

Use relevant illustrations and examples. Try to relate the content to the geographic and cultural setting of the institution. These examples should be appropriate for the content and the purpose of the lesson. Consider using examples that will create images in the minds of the students, ones they can almost feel, smell, and taste.

When you require homework, collect it and provide feedback in writing as soon as possible. The students put time and energy into their homework — they want to know that you respect them enough to read their work and to provide feedback.

Provide an advance organizer for the beginning of your presentation, e.g., "Today, we will discuss exponential functions." Advance organizers are broad, goal-oriented statements or assignments that help students establish a general mindset for what is about to happen during a lesson. A short reading assignment about the topic, but lacking specifics, would be an acceptable advance organizer.

Encourage the students to interact with you. Ask questions, then pause long enough for the students to organize a response — maybe 10 seconds. Acknowledge questions immediately. Many students have to muster up the courage to raise their hands and ask questions — strike while the iron is hot.

Praise students when they give appropriate answers: "That's a great response" or "That answer is particularly important because ... ." Be specific in your praise: be sure you show why the response is good. If a student gives an incorrect response, turn to another student and ask if he or she agrees and why. The student giving the incorrect response is less likely to feel embarrassed than if you simply say that he or she is wrong.

All of the above suggestions set the climate for the entire semester. The journey through the semester begins with a single step. Take that first step carefully and the journey will be much easier and more productive for everyone.

Deciding on strategies

I believe the following five major interacting variables within the classroom will determine to a great extent how successful your lessons will be:

1. All of your characteristics, e.g., personality, knowledge, skills, and experiences

2. All of the characteristics of your students, e.g., prerequisite knowledge and skills, personality, and attitude toward the subject under study

3. The structure of the knowledge, e.g., linear or non-linear

4. The classroom setting, e.g., movable chairs and tables versus stationary furniture, small class versus large class

5. Your instructional strategies

You should vary your teaching strategies to suit the objectives established for the lessons. One instructor might use a case study or simulation one day while another uses discussion.

How do you determine which strategies to use?

Remember the section in this book on determining objectives. Ask, "What do I want the students to be able to do at the end of today's lesson that they probably can't do before the lesson?" Then, once you've identified the daily objectives, ask, "Which instructional strategies will probably be best in helping the students reach my objectives for today's lesson?"

- If your objectives include a lot of factual information, lectures may be quite appropriate.

- If your objectives include affective behavior (values, attitudes), role-playing and simulation may be more effective than lecturing.

- If your objectives involve the manipulation of science equipment (psychomotor skills), provide opportunities for the students to use the equipment. A lecture would again be inappropriate, although a very short introductory and motivating mini-lecture might be essential (e.g., a type of "Don't blow us up today by mixing the wrong chemicals" introduction to using the equipment, as you demonstrate the correct procedures).

- If your objectives involve group dynamics, you would want to consider experiences that call for group activities.

- If your objectives include a review of previous content, you might want to use a strategy in which you ask questions about the subject and the students have to respond to those questions.

Your personality and learning style will be influential in helping you decide which approach to use for the various objectives. Galbraith and Sanders (1987) reported a high correlation between preferred learning styles of instructors and their preferred instructional methods. In other words, most instructors tend to teach their courses as they would take them: the teacher thinks as a student. This is certainly normal — but we should be aware of how our learning determines our teaching.

Ask a colleague or a departmental student advisor about the level of preparation and ability expected of students in the course. Note which curricula are heavily represented in your class. This information, available from class rosters or student introductions, may point to prior student preparation in your subject area. It can help you select among examples and make assignments that relate to students' experiences.

When communicating basic facts, the lecture approach is the standard strategy at the postsecondary level. However, there are a number of very different strategies that you should begin to add to your repertoire. (I will discuss several of the strategies in the next few chapters.)

Assume that you have listed your objectives and identified a number of different strategies that you could use to achieve the objectives. What do you do next?

Based on your knowledge of your students and how they might best learn the content associated with the objectives, select those strategies that appear to be better for the majority of your students (see MSLQ below). Also, consider any economic factors by answering the following question: "How much money will be required for the strategy (buying audiotapes, developing color slides, printing or buying a simulation program, renting a movie) and how much of my time (also an economic factor) will be required to prepare the lesson?" Then, answer another question: "Do I need additional space, microcomputers, study carrels, staff, and materials to make my strategies work?"

If I had to select one guideline that supersedes all others, I would have to choose *learning* — how students learn must be the central focus when selecting a strategy. We are teaching so that students learn. As obvious as this assumption might seem, many instructors believe otherwise: "I just tell the students the facts; it's up to them to learn" — as if *telling* and *teaching* are synonymous.

Using the MSLQ to help you determine strategies

A group of researchers associated with the National Center for Research to Improve Postsecondary Teaching and Learning (NCRIPTAL) developed a diagnostic tool — the Motivated Strategies for Learning Questionnaire (MSLQ) — to assess the learning styles of students and gain insight into student motivation for learning (Pintrich *et al.*, 1988). Another NCRIPTAL group developed a set of instructional strategies that overlay the MSLQ (Johnson *et al.*, 1991).

I believe instructors can administer the MSLQ in their classrooms, using computer-scoring answer sheets, to obtain a good snapshot of where the students fall among the 15 categories of the instrument. This diagnostic approach might help you select strategies appropriate to the course and lesson objectives and the basic motivational needs of most of your students. How?

The next several pages provide examples of how you could use several of the MSLQ categories to help you with instructional strategies for various lessons. Most of the suggestions, as indicated in parentheses, come from Cross and Angelo (1988), *Classroom Assessment Techniques: A Handbook for Faculty*, an excellent guide. The titles they use to describe the examples are given in the parentheses.

Rehearsal strategies

Here is a strategy detailed by Cross and Angelo ("Focused Listing") that might help students who are weak in a certain area. You could have the students list information they believe other students should know to be successful on a forthcoming examination. Why? The students are actively involved, and their statements can serve as feedback to you, so that you can determine how much information the students can recall. Ask the students to share their information during group sessions. Develop a set of topics and distribute the list to the students to review, either in groups or alone, if gaps in knowledge are apparent.

Selection strategies

You could have the students recall important information covered in the course, then ask them to categorize the information ("Memory Matrix"). (Cross and Angelo note that this strategy is most useful "in courses with a high information content, such as courses in the natural sciences, foreign languages, music theory, history, or law.") Why? The students are actively using their thought processes while you are assessing their ability to recall and organize information covered in the course. Have students list the information that would fit into a matrix in which the categories have been listed as headings (see example on the next page), then fill in the matrix.

**Example: Memory Matrix Contrasting Positive
and Negative Statements**

	Positive	Negative
At home		
At school		

Another approach to use with Selection Strategies ("Background Knowledge Probes") consists of finding out what the students already know prior to introducing new material. You can use this technique to determine what information to emphasize and what information to cover in less detail, because you'll be analyzing the students' knowledge and comprehension levels. You could develop a survey questionnaire that includes basic information in the material to be presented.

The following is an example of a question that might guide your preparation for a session on evaluation and assessment: "Do the students have a thorough understanding of the terms *mean, median,* and *mode*?" Ask the students to describe their understanding of each of the terms.

Another example ("Focused Dialectical Notes") involves analysis skills. Distribute two articles having divergent views about the same topic and ask the students to write a critical analysis. Why? You can compare the students' notes with a set of notes you have developed, then provide feedback to the students if they misunderstood the content of the articles or failed to locate important information.

You could also have students analyze the notes taken by other students. Why? Students hear the same statements in different ways. When students interact with other students about the instructor's presentation, they have a better opportunity to clarify their notes. Near the end of the class session, you could divide the students into groups and have each group summarize its notes.

Elaboration strategies

You could tell students to describe in their own words the material covered in a lecture or assigned reading, to paraphrase important information in writing ("Directed Paraphrasing"). Why? Students will better understand how well they have grasped the more important elements in a lecture or assigned reading if you collect their summaries and provide them with feedback.

You could engage the students in a structured written assignment ("Analytic Memos"). Why? The activity actively involves students as they develop their analytic and writing skills.

Divide the class into two groups, and assign each group a different problem. Have one group of students role-play executives, managers, or political analysts who scrutinize the memos written by the other group of students. You should identify the role of the students, the audience for the memo, deadline for completion of the memo, and length of the memo (usually two or three pages). You should probably write a memo for each assignment and then compare elements included in your memo with those by the students. After reading the students' memos, you can provide feedback.

Metacognition strategies

You could have the students describe the steps they used in solving a problem ("Documented Problem-Set Solutions"). Why? This activity forces the students to think about the information processing they have used to reach a conclusion. After demonstrating your own problem-solving process, you can provide a situation that would be new to the students, then direct them to write down the steps they used to solve the problem.

You could provide a written assignment that requires the students to use critical reading skills ("Do & Say [Function & Content] Analysis"). Why? Students must develop critical reading skills to help them analyze what they read. You can have the students outline a chapter in the textbook or the content in a handbook. You can then review their outlines to see if they can identify the important elements in the material while they are paraphrasing. It would be helpful if you would provide feedback to the students about their critical reading skills.

Organization strategies

You could have the students categorize a set of items drawn from class lectures and/or assigned readings ("The Defining Feature Matrix"). Why? Students become actively involved with a process that helps them store information for retrieval at a later date. Provide a list of important items; ask the students to place the items inside a matrix. For example, a set of terms could be listed along the left side of a matrix and category labels could appear across the top; the students could place a check mark at the proper intersection of a term and a category label.

Another organization strategy ("One-Sentence Summaries [WDWW HWWW]") would be to engage the students in creatively summarizing a topic. Why? Students need to learn techniques that will help them summarize information into smaller units so that they can better recall the information at a later date.

Cross and Angelo present a structure for such summarizing, which they claim can be used to summarize almost everything that is represented in the declarative form. Students first complete a matrix in which the left column is labeled "Question" and the right column is labeled "Response." The students respond to the following questions: Who? Do What? To What or Whom? How? When? Where? Why? (WDWWHWWW) After completing the matrix, the students must use the data in the response column to summarize the information in sentence form.

Original thinking

This category usually involves the skill of synthesizing. You could have the students write a prospectus ("The Paper or Project Prospectus"). Why? Students need to strengthen their synthesizing skills so that they can more creatively plan their projects for the course. Require the students to complete a detailed plan for a class paper or project. Include such elements as topic, purpose of the topic, identification of the audience, questions to be answered, general organization, and required resources.

You could have the students connect their original thinking to course content ("Annotated Portfolios of Creative Work"). Why? Students are actively and creatively involved in using the information they have gained from the content. Cross and Angelo believe that having students maintain a file of their creative work is particularly suited to courses in the visual arts, painting, architecture, poetry, journalism, creative writing, clinical fields, drawing, music, drama, dance, fashion, and broadcasting. Direct the students to maintain samples of their work in folders, and ask them to describe in their own words the relationship between the samples and the content of the course.

Intrinsic goal orientation

You could attempt to identify the learning goals of the students ("Student Goals Ranking"). Why? You can identify how closely the learning goals of the students correspond to the learning goals for the course. You could tell the students to rank the objectives in the course syllabus in line with their personal perceptions of the importance of each goal. This activity requires each student to assess his or her personal learning goals with your course-specific instructional goals.

You could ask the students to determine how successful they think they will be in your course ("Course-Related Interest and Skills Checklist"). Why? Students will better understand what they need to do to complete the course. You could provide a checklist of topics covered in the course and the skills needed to successfully complete the course; students would indicate how well-prepared they are to master the topics and which skills they think they lack.

Expectations of success

You could have the students describe a specific classroom learning experience they have had since entering college ("Focused Autobiographical Sketches of Students as Learners"). Why? This forces students to look at themselves as learners; it also helps you assess their perceptions of their success in learning. Ask the students to write a one- or two-page sketch of themselves as learners during one specific experience.

You could have the students evaluate their current levels of learning from different points of view ("Dual-Viewpoint Skills Portraits"). Why? It makes them more self-aware and it allows you to appreciate the extent to which the self-assessments agree with your assessments. Have the students make a presentation, complete a writing assignment, videotape their own performances, or any other class project. Next, have them describe their effectiveness or ineffectiveness in completing the assignment, from two different points of view — their own and a fellow student's.

Help-seeking behavior

If the students and you have access to electronic mail services, Cross and Angelo suggest the following strategy ("Student-Teacher Electronic Mail Messages"). Use the system to write an open letter to the students, then encourage them to respond, keeping their responses personal and confidential. They do not need to share them with other students. Why? This is one of the more non-threatening ways for students to express frustrations that you may or may not sense. Include a few questions about your teaching or a difficult session or topic that the students may have encountered in the course. Analyze their responses and follow up with appropriate actions and comments.

Determining your focus

Does making learning the central focus of your teaching make for more work? You bet! You must rethink the various theories and models of learning for clues about how best to present material to your students:

- Do you want to emphasize discovery?

- Do you want to stress operation processes?

- Do you have a behaviorist view that emphasizes stimulus-response theory?

- Do you support human modeling that stresses vicarious reinforcement?

- Do you need to administer a learning questionnaire to a typical group of students who will be taking your course, so that you can find out more about their learning styles?

You may find the above questions overwhelming at this time in your career; however, I believe you should begin to give such questions more of your time. You are beginning your teaching career — you have many years ahead in which to delve into the above in more depth.

Problem attitudes and behaviors

The best intentions, plans, and strategies can be undermined if students exhibit problem attitudes and behaviors. Downs (1992) provides some guidance for dealing with hostile students and offers eight suggestions:

1. Ask yourself if you've done anything to contribute to the conflict.

2. Confer with the student one on one in a neutral setting.

3. Find common ground.

4. Try a series of cooperative learning exercises and discuss social skills.

5. Try not to take attacks personally or become defensive.

6. Talk with colleagues about similar situations and how they handle them.

7. Integrate problem-solving and conflict resolution activities into your regular lessons.

8. Use direct confrontation as a last resort.

Critical thinking

It seems that critical thinking is on almost every educator's list of priorities. But how can you move from idealism to reality?

Adams (1993) describes four techniques he uses to help students develop as critical thinkers:

1. *A mini-research project* that permits students to research a question or idea that wasn't covered in depth during class time

2. *A scenario-based research project* that allows the student to assume a role in which it is his or her responsibility to explain pros and cons of a process or new equipment (e.g., role playing a consultant interacting with the manager of a factory)

3. *A short essay question* above the recall level of the subject matter

4. An issues-directed research project that requires the students to fullly investigate an issue or process

Newton (1991) discusses the use of a "response journal": students chronicle and judge their own work, thus gaining a better understanding of their own metacognitive strategies.

Remember: critical thinking is not something that you teach and your students learn, but rather a way of focusing your teaching and their learning. Your students may not long remember specific information they learn in your courses, but they should benefit in many ways from your efforts to help them develop their ability to think.

How to Lecture More Effectively

Since instructors continue to select the lecture more than any other instructional strategy, I think we should begin with techniques that will improve your style of lecturing. As Clarke (1987, p. 54) observes,

> Successful lecturers often succeed because they leave room for students to react, encourage reaction, and scan the audience for clues about the health of the interaction. They know the reaction to look for and take steps to ensure that reaction.

But how do we leave room for reactions? How do we encourage students? What clues can serve to guide us? And how do we ensure proper reactions from our students?

We know the following advantages of the lecture approach:

- We believe it is time-efficient.
- We can reuse the lecture in different sections of the same course, and we can repeat the lecture from semester to semester.
- We feel comfortable because we know that the content has been presented.
- We can provide organization, particularly if the structure of the knowledge is linear.
- We can highlight major facts, concepts, principles, and generalizations that students might overlook in their reading.

McLeish (1976) justified the use of the lecture by discussing five reasons for using the strategy:

1. Students are too immature or unresponsive to learn via self-directed reading, on their own.
2. We can reach very large numbers of students.

3. The instructor can go over the material in a textbook, using different words and illustrations to clarify concepts and understandings.

4. Complex scientific information that hasn't been published in textbooks can be introduced.

5. The instructor can be the "critic" of the material in the textbook.

Lectures center around complex knowledge. Weinstein and Hamman (1994, p. 57) declare:

> Instruction that builds from simple to complex knowledge coupled with processing skills can have a tremendous impact on moving students along the novice to expert continuum — they may not all become experts, but we can certainly have an impact on their level of expertise.

Weinstein and Hamman go on to state that it is important to help students see how the material will help them in the future (p. 59). They also encourage the use of discussion, a topic I will address later.

Lectures also have limitations. Instructors may simply read the materials or present the information in a boring manner or with a monotonous voice. The lecture format may prevent students from becoming actively involved for the entire class session. How can we overcome such limitations of the lecture?

Be knowledgeable

Remain knowledgeable about the content you are teaching. Attend seminars and conferences where others are presenting similar content. Take notes during their presentations, paying particular attention to new ideas and new research information. Read the journals in your discipline. Ask publishing companies for review copies of new textbooks.

Develop a scheme for taking down important information presented in the journals and textbooks. If you find a particularly good schematic drawing or graph, write to the author and the journal or textbook publisher and ask for permission to make a transparency copy of the page to use in your class. Be aware of copyright laws. You should use this approach only on a limited basis. (If you ask, most publishers will send you a summary of the copyright laws or direct you to a source.) Develop an appropriate system for storing your notes and related materials, so that you can easily retrieve such items when you need them for classes or for revising your course.

Reviewing and revising your lectures is another way to remain knowledgeable; students joke about instructors who bring to class their yellowed sheets of lecture notes that have coffee stains and frayed edges.

All of these preliminary activities will create an air of confidence when you enter the classroom.

Systematic preparation

You will want to develop a structure for your lectures. They shouldn't be simply a flow of information chopped into time chunks. Clarke (1987, p. 52) offers some suggestions that will help you to accomplish this:

- Select your topic.
- Develop a question that serves as a guide. Pose your question at the start of your lecture, then answer it at the end: "Recall the question I raised at the beginning of today's class ... ." Repeat the question, then give a one-statement thesis.
- List the important parts, steps, and elements of the lecture's thesis.
- Collect media items — charts, maps, photographs, transparencies, slides — that will help communicate the thesis.
- Identify key details to include in the lecture.
- Summarize the thesis. Make a list of important facts, concepts, principles, generalizations, and happenings that contributed in some way to the thesis you are presenting.

Outline the lecture

An outline of the lecture is essential for several reasons:

- It provides a snapshot of the entire lecture. When you review the topic headings and subheadings prior to class, it gives you more confidence and a better idea of how the class session will flow.
- It helps keep you on track.
- It allows you to estimate better how much time will be needed to deliver the lecture.
- You can insert questions at key points in the outline.

- You can give the students copies of the outline to help them follow the lecture and to use when reviewing for quizzes and examinations.

- You can rehearse your lecture while following your outline; you could audiotape the practice session and make necessary adjustments.

Use facts early in the lecture, then end with higher-level reasoning that leads students to conclusions. By opening the lecture with a thesis question and following with a series of related facts and events that serve as a flight of stairs, you can guide the students as they climb to the higher cognitive levels of application, analysis, synthesis, and problem-solving.

Use questions to stimulate interaction in large classes. Queries with one-word or two-word answers can get the students started. Directing questions to the class in general, instead of singling out individuals to respond, seems the better approach. When a student mumbles a response, repeat it for the other students. In mid-lecture, ask the class to take five minutes to pose questions — and if the questions are good, say so!

Near the end of the lecture, direct the students to take two minutes to write out a question over the day's content — one they believe might appear on an examination. Collect and review their questions before the next class session; when you find a good one, use it to modify your next presentation — so that the students take the two-minute question session seriously.

Establish rapport with your class

The success of your lecture might depend on how well you have established the classroom climate. Calling students by name, reflecting a positive attitude, using humor, and even taking class pictures can help build rapport with the class.

Begin to identify as many students by name as possible. You could make a seating chart during the first day of class and write down the names of the students as they introduce themselves. Some instructors like to bring a camera to class and take pictures of the students in groups of five. They then circulate the photos and have the students write their names under their faces. Then, when students raise questions during lectures, the instructors can refer to the photos and call on the students by name, building images of the students throughout the semester.

The more positive you can be, the more likely it is that the students will react favorably to your presentations. Positive reinforcement strengthens learning: praise students when they provide good answers to questions. However, avoid praising everything and praising generically; some instructors get into the habit of saying "Good answer" or "Good idea" to every comment from their students, who soon realize the praise is empty.

Studies have shown that humor can increase student attention while providing examples that promote learning (Powell and Andresen, 1985). Korobkin (1988, p. 155) lists several "alleged benefits" in the use of humor:

- Retention of material
- Student-teacher rapport
- Attentiveness and interest
- Motivation toward and satisfaction with learning
- Playfulness and positive attitude
- Individual and group task productivity
- Class discussion and animation
- Creativity, idea generation, and divergent thinking

Korobkin states that humor decreases:

- Academic stress
- Anxiety toward subject matter
- Dogmatism
- Class monotony

Spontaneous humor — when instructors and students laugh together — is desirable, while malicious humor that ridicules students or races or genders or beliefs is undesirable.

Parrott (1994) reported having a "long-standing interest in the use of humor, as a coping tool, as part of a positive outlook on life and practice, and as a teaching strategy" (p. 37). She reports that she has long used many forms of humor with her nursing students. She shares two basic questions that she always asks herself:

- Does this method/strategy help decrease student anxiety — in testing, laboratory check-offs, patient care, and future practice?
- Does this method/strategy help the students retain and transfer content and concepts from the classroom to the practice setting?

She also alerts us to the fact (p. 37) that we

must be careful when using humor ... to avoid some of the pitfalls, such as ridicule, sarcasm, and racist or ethnic jokes. It is important to be able to laugh with someone, not at them, so as not to offend them. The wrong kind of humor can be demeaning and destroy self-esteem and confidence, interfere with communication, and sever relationships.

Studies are revealing the benefits derived when instructors interact with students and when students interact with other students. You can pause during the lecture and ask a question about the content covered during the previous five or ten minutes. You can break the lecture and have students engage in small group discussions when the lecture has taken them to the edge of a problem-solving situation.

These can be refreshing and productive changes of pace for the students and you. Gullette (1992) stresses the importance of breaks during lecturing so that discussions can be intermixed with lecture. Geske (1992) suggests using a "Donahue" method by role-playing to alleviate some limitations of the large lecture arena.

Creating a lively lecture

When you do it well, Frederick (1986, p. 44) notes, the lecture can:

- Impart new information

- Explain, clarify, and organize difficult concepts

- Model a creative mind at work or in the problem-solving process

- Analyze and show relationships among seemingly dissimilar ideas

- Inspire a reverence for learning

- Challenge beliefs and habits of thinking

- Breed enthusiasm and motivation for further study

Frederick claims that there are at least eight variations on the lecture that can make it more lively:

1. **The Exquisite Oral Essay.** This finely tuned presentation deals with one intellectual question or problem, has unity, and is "introduced, illustrated, and concluded within 50 minutes" (p. 45). The instructor conveys only the important information. An example would be a lecture devoted entirely to Robert E. Lee's experiences at the military academy before the Civil War.

2. **The Participatory Lecture.** With this approach, students are encouraged to develop "ideas which are then organized in some rational, coherent pattern on the chalkboard" (p. 45). The instructor could list the events leading up to the Civil War as the students suggest them. Once the list has been exhausted, items that appear to have similarities could be grouped together. Labels or titles could be created for each group of events: "How would you label these three events?" The groups could be reorganized by titles on a timeline, from the earliest set of events to the final group just prior to the outbreak of the Civil War.

3. **Problem-solving: Demonstrations, proofs, and stories.** Opening with a question can catch the students' attention. You then develop the answer throughout the class session. The solution "may require a scientific demonstration, a mathematical proof, an economic model, the outcome of the novel's plot, or an historical narrative" (pp. 46-47). For example, an instructor might begin a lecture with the following:

> When Franklin Roosevelt returned from the Yalta Conference near the close of World War II, news films depicted a crew of Secret Service men lifting him out of a railway car while he lay on a stretcher. Was he near death? Had he been injured during the return trip from Yalta? Had he been stricken with an illness? Why was he on a stretcher?

The instructor builds the lecture around Roosevelt's early political career, when he was suddenly struck with polio, an illness that caused him to devote much of his effort to eradicating the disease — by creating The March of Dimes.

4. **Energy shifts: Alternating mini-lectures and discussions.** The instructor sets the stage with a 15- to 20-minute lecture, followed by 10 to 15 minutes of discussion. A new topic is introduced during another 15- to 20-minute lecture, followed by 10 to 15 minutes of discussion. The instructor gives the students an assignment at the close of the class session, and the next class session begins with a mini-discussion of that assignment.

5. **Textual exegesis: Modeling analytical skills.** This approach can be used in courses as varied as the history of art, music, economics, anthropology, science, social science, and English. It is a process of analytical modeling:

> A class of 50 or 500 students, following along in their books, or on handouts, or on an overhead projection,

can watch a professor working through selected passages of a document, speech, sermon, essay, poem, proof, or fictional passage (p. 47).

For example, an instructor directs the students to a certain page in the basic textbook, then "thinks aloud" as the students read the page. The instructor demonstrates his or her learning style by talking while skimming through the page of the text.

6. **Cutting large classes in half without losing control: Debates.** A classroom of students can be divided into two sides by using a center aisle. Half of the students support one side of an issue while the other half support a different view:

> From the right side of the hall we will hear five statements on behalf of the Confederacy, after which we will hear five statements from the left on behalf of the Union (p. 48).

You could even create a middle ground for those students who wish to remain neutral, but you need to encourage this group to defend its neutrality with reasonable explanations. It would be advisable to provide the students with ample background information and materials prior to the day of the debate. I like to inform the students in advance that they must be prepared to defend both sides of the issue; nobody knows until the day of the debate which half of the room will represent which side of the issue.

7. **Smaller groups in large classes: Simulations and role-playing.** After a mini-lecture, organize the students into small groups. Give each group an explicit role and a specific task to pursue. You can conclude the class by incorporating the solutions or suggestions flowing from each group. Or you might instruct the groups to "prepare speeches and see the deliberations through to some conclusion, or to caucus in order to develop strategies, coalitions, and tactics for achieving their goals" (p. 49).

8. **Bells and whistles: The affective, emotional media lecture.** Frederick describes two approaches "designed to evoke an emotional involvement by affective, emotional learning, an area woefully neglected in college teaching" (p. 49).

One uses a series of dramatic quotations, poems, or lyrics that focus on a specific topic, perhaps read by some theater arts majors. For example, when working with the Pythagorean theorem in mathematics, three students could play the roles of Socrates, Meno, and Meno's slave while they read from the dialogues of Plato. The remainder of the students watch how the dialogue unfolds as Socrates demonstrates to Meno how an uneducated slave can be taught a mathematical theorem simply through a series of questions raised by Socrates.

The second approach uses a slide-tape presentation. I use a form of this approach each spring term, in a college curriculum course. I use the strategy during the week that we celebrate Martin Luther King's birthday. I close the class session by announcing that we will discuss teaching ethics as part of the college curriculum during next week's class, and I ask them to listen, watch, and then leave the classroom without talking, but to remember how the session ended as they prepare for next week's class. I then play an audiotape of King's "I Have a Dream."

Aspects of delivery

Any of the above variations on the lecture will provide variety and keep students interested in your course. Here are some final suggestions when using the lecture approach:

1. Know your subject matter. You must reflect a knowledge of your discipline. You communicate your interest in the subject by remaining up to date. Toss out the old material and keep adding new information.

2. Speak slowly, loudly, and clearly, aiming your words at all areas of the room. Students shouldn't have to strain to hear you. Vary the pitch and tone of your voice.

3. Look at the students, not at the blackboard, floor, or ceiling. You pick up many cues from the expressions on the faces of the students.

4. Constantly pursue answers to questions about what worked, what didn't work, and what might work the next time you deliver the lecture. Reflect on the last class session. Try to visualize the flow of the lecture and the reactions of the students.

5. Be prepared — but be alive, spontaneous. There is something positive about spontaneity in the classroom that keeps the students attentive. Spontaneity is an art to develop. You want to be

prepared, but not so much that you squelch spontaneity. Provide illustrations and examples from current events.

6. Move your body as well as your mouth; don't take up a fixed posture at a podium. Students question the confidence and preparation of instructors who stand with white knuckles at a podium day after day. You may want to seek advice and counsel from instructors in speech communication and theater arts.

7. Summarize at the end of the lecture.

Murray and Murray (1992) provide a lecture model that includes:

- Anticipation (setting the stage with overall issues, desired outcomes)

- Preparation (selecting materials, deciding on delivery systems, obtaining needed resources, designing the format)

- Delivering the lecture (thinking about time, speech habits, demeanor, and body language)

- Evaluating the outcome of the lecture

King (1992) found that if she trained students in advance in self-questioning and summarizing, those students learned more from lectures than students without such training.

Overholser (1992) focuses on the need to engage students in active learning. He claims that the traditional lecture doesn't encourage thought processes. He states, "In contrast to the usual methods, Socratic approaches use thought content to change thought processes" (p. 14). He elaborates on each of his "Elements of the Socratic Methods in Teaching," using the acronym "SOCRATIC":

S: systematic questioning

O: objective and critical thinking

C: collaborative investigation

R: rational problem-solving

A: active participation

T: tested hypotheses

I: inductive reasoning

C: comprehensive generalities

Overholser closes his article by stating that the elements "are very appropriate to classroom settings and can promote an active learning environment in which students learn to evaluate information and develop a more sophisticated approach to various problems" (p. 18).

Moving from
"Sage on the Stage"
to
"Guide on the Side"

The lecture approach lends itself to the presentation of basic facts and basic information. However, when students have the appropriate knowledge and your objectives suggest a strategy other than the lecture, there are a number of approaches to choose that help shift the environment from teacher-centered to learner-centered, that allow you to be less a "sage on the stage" and more a "guide on the side." Alternatives include:

- Discussions
- Term papers
- Oral reports
- Peer groups
- Case studies
- Simulations and role play
- Multi-media presentations
- Blackboard techniques
- Field trips
- Individualized plans and self-pacing
- Lab experiences
- Microcomputer programs

Discussions as a systematic way to encourage interaction

Discussions are best suited for objectives that deal with higher cognitive processes and problem-solving activities. They usually motivate better than lectures — although a dynamic and well-orchestrated lecture will probably be more motivational than a poorly planned and disorganized discussion. You should consider using the discussion approach when your objectives include having students formulate and solve problems, providing them with an opportunity to judge their own perceptions against the perceptions of classmates, and using the diverse experiences of the students to accentuate a point.

You may have problems with shy students or students who tend to react more slowly. Hansen (1987, p. 59) offers a suggestion:

> You might ask a question, but offer the student a chance to prepare an answer while the rest of the class discusses something else for, say, five minutes. This combines respect for the student's ability to handle a useful issue with a soothing offer of time to compose the nerves.

Of course, the student may miss something important or feel different from the others. As with almost all decisions in the classroom, it's a judgment call.

Duell (1994) experimented with "wait time" following questions and reported that three to five seconds would be adequate in most cases when dealing with higher-order questions.

Cooperative learning

Cooperative learning is not easy to define; there are many variations, instructional strategies, and classroom activities that deserve to be included in any descriptions of cooperative learning. Miles and Stubblefield (1982) believe group learning is beneficial for students: "Unlike many other techniques, learning groups offer opportunities for learners to be involved actively in the process, to make use of their own experience, and to assume responsibility for their own learning" (p. 311).

Students might:

- Work in small groups to prepare reports, which they would present in the classroom

- Serve as peer mentors or tutors to help others develop writing skills or conduct science experiments

- Work with faculty members on research topics

Whipple (1987) notes the following characteristics of cooperative learning:

- It involves instructors and students participating in an active learning experience.

- It bridges the chasm between instructor and students if the instructor collaborates with the students in the formative stages of the task to be pursued; this promotes active dialogue between instructors and students.

- It involves a sense of community: *cooperation* takes precedence over *competitiveness*. Cooperation is an important skill for students to acquire before entering the world of work. Students should learn to respect the differences that exist among the members of any group.

- It involves developing information, because cooperation requires the use of interactive processes.

- It brings teaching and research together. Classrooms become the research laboratories for creating knowledge.

- It recreates and refashions old knowledge into new forms: the knowledge emerges from the social interactions among the participants, and it lives in the community of students who are involved in cooperative learning. "It is a common misconception," Whipple asserts, "that collaborative beliefs about knowledge ignore the value of each knower's contribution. Rather, in a collaborative situation involving, say, six persons, there are seven distinct knowledges represented — those of each individual and that of the group as a collective entity" (p. 5).

Some examples of cooperative learning:

> **Example A:** A physical chemistry instructor obtained background information from all of the students in the course, then divided them into groups, mixing chemistry and engineering majors. He assigned them a reading, conducted group discussions, tested the students, engaged them in group discussions of the test, organized group activities such as cases and role-playing, and finally presented a culminating lecture.

> **Example B:** Some instructors use "learning cells" or "dyads" that stress cooperative learning in pairs. Students read an assignment, then write questions dealing with major

facts, concepts, etc. At the beginning of the next class session, the students are randomly assigned to pairs. Partner A asks partner B the first question. After B answers and perhaps receives corrections, B asks A the next question, and so on. The instructor moves from dyad to dyad, asking questions and providing feedback.

The success of cooperative learning depends on several factors, including understanding the process, engaging the students in meaningful group activities, and planning before implementing the assignment.

A math instructor tried cooperative learning in a calculus class (Kaiser, 1988). The results were disastrous.

Does that sound familiar? We hear or read about new strategies that have been successful for someone else, but then they don't work for us.

Well, this math instructor didn't blame the strategy when she failed. She immediately reflected on the experience and identified the causes for the failure — students were tired, she hadn't prepared them for the activity, and she really didn't know how to implement cooperative learning.

She learned more about the process — that small, informal work groups spend only five to ten minutes together, while more formal cooperative learning groups work until a specific job is completed, sometimes for several weeks.

Now armed with basic knowledge, she prepared her students long before she tried cooperative learning again. She told her calculus students that they had to read the material in advance of class, and she explained that the class would combine tiny lectures with short tasks that they had to complete in groups of two. When the students completed the assignment, the instructor reported that the class session was a great success!

She was surprised that they managed to cover all the materials they had to cover, and she noted that the students' energy levels were very high throughout the activity. She also received enthusiastic responses from the students when she queried them about their interest in the cooperative learning approach.

Kaiser notes (p. 3):

> By using class time to have the partners discuss a new assignment (instead of my lecturing about it), I've noticed a big improvement in the finished programs. And by moving around the room to answer a group's questions and to keep discussions going, I have time to

challenge the brighter students and encourage the slower students without embarrassing anyone.

She also reports another interesting observation. She claims that those students who were enrolled in calculus only because there wasn't any other course were slightly unhappy — because they discovered that they had to participate instead of just passing time in her classroom!

Friedlander and MacDougall (1992) report on a strong and positive relationship between student involvement and achievement. Keller (1993) believes that students learn to read with greater purpose and are more motivated to enter into discussions when they are working in cooperative learning settings.

Others reporting success with cooperative learning include Lawrence (1991), Karabenick and Knapp (1991), Hawkes (1992), Sheridan, Byrne, and Quina (1989), Bredehoft (1991), Beckman (1990), Lidren, Meier, and Brigham (1991), Lundy (1991), and Petonito (1991). And Saunders (1992) reviews recent developments and encouragement involving student-centered activities in postsecondary settings in the United Kingdom, with peer tutoring being one of the experiments at Nottingham Polytechnic.

Critical thinking

Browne and Keeley (1988) declared that many students lack critical thinking skills, concluding (p. 2),

> To improve the thinking skills of students, professors should be aware that the traditional curricula do not guarantee the internalization of critical thinking skills. Direct training, combined with practice and reinforcement, is needed to facilitate the development of critical thinking skills.

Can we assess critical thinking if we can't see it? We can observe learners' critical thinking behavior as reflected during a classroom discussion. We can critique students' products generated by critical thinking outside the classroom, such as a term paper. Critical thinking might be reflected in the development of three-dimensional models.

According to Brookfield (1987), critical thinking involves the dual processes of "identifying and challenging assumptions" and "imagining and exploring alternatives" (p. 229). He lists the following generalizations about critical thinking (pp. 231-233):

- The processes involved are person-specific.

- Emotions play a major role.

- Both intrinsic and extrinsic reasons are important.

- It can occur unexpectedly.

- Peer support is important.

There are many ways to encourage students to develop their critical thinking skills. Brookfield provides an excellent set of conclusions to help guide us in facilitating critical thinking (pp. 233-235):

- No one model of critical thinking stands out as a panacea; intervening variables involving people and contexts make it impossible to propose one standard model for all uses.

- We must provide a variety of methods and materials for diverse learners.

- We shouldn't expect perfection.

- We shouldn't look at "learner satisfaction" as the primary criterion for judging the level of success of a critical thinking activity. Sometimes we need periods of frustration, and sometimes we need to struggle to find potential solutions to problems.

- We need to take risks. That entails the possibility of failure, but we should not stop our efforts simply because of one attempt that is less than successful.

Browne and Keeley-Vasudeva (1992) urge the use of controversy during classroom time to force students to think critically. Garland (1991) uses controversial issues and groups students into point-counterpoint teams that present both sides of the controversy during class time. Jackson (1991) used the banning of *Huckleberry Finn* as the center for a debate to foster critical thinking. Jennings (1993) provides an example of critical thinking for a geography class: an exercise is designed to bring students into contact with an urban landscape, to help them better understand the thinking that must go into designing an urban environment.

Field studies

Field study methodology, according to Wulff and Nyquist (1988), is an instructional tool that enhances critical thinking. Field studies are usually long-term and are not the same as short field trips. Students "observe, analyze, classify and report human behavior occurring in natural environments" (p. 87).

Wulff and Nyquist describe one approach to field study in which the instructor had students compare and contrast the findings from their observations with those from readings and lectures. Students were to present tentative hypotheses and conclusions to their peers. The activity, which included small group discussions, encouraged synthesis.

The instructor wanted the students to perform as researchers and arranged for a presentation by a researcher experienced in field methods. The presentation included information on taking notes in the field, what to include in the record, separating observations and inferences, formulating hypotheses, analyzing and classifying information into categories, identifying themes, and presenting and supporting conclusions with specific findings from field notes (p. 91).

Hess (1988) engages her business students in "thinking about thinking" exercises. She believes that such experiences are essential if business students are to succeed in the real world. In her effort to discover protocols that identify steps, skills, processes, and behaviors involved in such mental activities as reasoning, decision-making, problem-solving, learning-to-learn, and critical and creative thinking, she rediscovered the Taxonomy of Educational Objectives (Bloom *et al.*, 1956).

When Hess introduces some course content, she has the students reference a handout that lists the following six levels of the cognitive domain:

- Knowledge
- Comprehension
- Application
- Analysis
- Synthesis
- Evaluation

The handout includes "a key word, a thinking process, teaching goals, student behaviors, and typical words ... that require thinking at that level" (p. 2). The students refer to the handout and then think about each of Bloom's levels, which are then demonstrated by the instructor and practiced by the students.

Powers and Enright (1987) wanted to identify which reasoning skills faculty perceived as most critical for students to succeed in graduate schools. They noted that when faculty members were asked to identify important reasoning skills, the most highly rated critical thinking skills involved reasoning or problem-solving when needed information was not known, the ability to identify fallacies and contradictions in arguments, and noting similarities between types of problems or theories. They also identified the three most serious errors in reasoning: inability to question assumptions, inability to integrate and synthesize the ideas obtained from a variety of sources, and inability to develop hypotheses independently.

Browne and Keeley (1988) asked a group of students to evaluate a 550-word essay. The essay had many errors of evidence, ambiguities, and assumptions, and important information was missing. More than 50% of the students did not question any of the ambiguities, and more than 50% failed to comment on a loose definition that was essential for the students to be able to draw accurate conclusions about the article.

In my "College Teaching" course, I provide a simulation experience in which the students are identified as first-year assistant professors at my institution; I serve as their department chair, regardless of the students' disciplines. I provide the students with real catalogues, rules and regulations, policy manuals, etc., and then give them a set of 20 "in-basket" items that are typical problems that all new instructors must handle.

The students have one hour to write down their course of action for each of the "in-basket" items: if they make phone calls, they must write out the conversation; if they want to send the secretary a note, they must write out the note; if they need to talk to me, they discover that I am in Houston and can't be reached — therefore, they write out their actions. Eventually the entire group of students is engaged in discussing the more critical issues they will probably confront in the real world.

It is very rewarding to observe the discussions, and I always prod here and there to force the students to reveal their decision-making processes. They soon begin to learn that critical thinking takes place within a context, that there are alternative courses of action that should be explored, that reflecting about and probing into others' reasons for actions can lead to valuable lessons, and that data collection precedes conclusions.

A team of researchers at the National Center for Research to Improve Postsecondary Teaching and Learning (NCRIPTAL) has developed a self-report instrument to evaluate the motivational orientation and learning strategies of college students (Pintrich et al., 1988). One section of the instrument deals with critical thinking. We can duplicate and distribute that section to our students, and we can take time to elaborate on the items during class time:

- When confronted with difficult problems, try to develop potential solutions — and then check out your hypothesized answers.

- When instructors present theories and generalizations, try to find good supporting evidence.

- When you read or hear an assertion or conclusion, think about potential alternatives.

- Instead of relying entirely on the instructor's ideas, develop your own understanding of topics you read or hear.

Using questions to enhance discussions

One of the criticisms of classroom instruction targets the failure of some teachers to engage students in the use of higher cognitive processes — to think. The Taxonomy of Educational Objectives (see Figure 1.1, p. 11) presents six levels of cognition: knowledge, comprehension, application, analysis, synthesis, and evaluation (Bloom *et al.*, 1956). You can use the four higher-level skills — application, analysis, synthesis, and evaluation — to guide you in developing questions to enhance discussions and engage students in thinking.

> **Application questions**. These questions have a broader scope than simple recall of information. The purpose of such questions is to lead the student to apply concepts, principles, or generalizations in different contexts. They can serve in various contexts:
>
> - Having read the *Dialogues of Plato*, how can you apply the teaching style of Socrates in your own classroom instruction?
>
> - Having discussed the research findings at the Hawthorne Plant of Western Electric, how would you behave as an administrator or manager in a similar plant that mass produces light fixtures?
>
> **Questions that call for analysis and synthesis**. These questions require students to draw on all the knowledge they have learned in order to apply the appropriate knowledge to a given situation:
>
> - Why does cotton grow better in the Brazos Valley than in the higher areas of the Big Bend country?

- What could a builder do with the land around the intersection of Highway 6 and Highway 10 if the swamps were drained?

Questions that require comparison of objects or statements. These questions force students to look for similarities and differences:

- How does the HP LaserJet II Printer differ from the IBM QuietWriter Printer Model 2?

- Are the editorials on the topic of energy different in *The New York Times* and *The Houston Chronicle*? Explain.

Questions that call for evaluation. Most of the time, there are no specific right or wrong answers for evaluation questions, and that makes the standards or criteria the instructor will use to judge the students' responses an important part of the pre-presentation strategy:

- Look at these two microscopes. Which is the better instrument, and why?

- Was U.S. Grant a better general than Robert E. Lee? Why?

Bloom contends that evaluation requires students to use some combination of the cognitive processes listed earlier — knowledge, comprehension, application, analysis, and synthesis.

Problem-solving questions. These questions challenge students to use their creativity in devising solutions to problems. It is this active involvement that enables students to more easily store information in long-term memory; the active involvement may also make it easier for the students to retrieve information from long-term memory at a later date.

For example:

- Form groups of five and reference your notes and the new handouts I distributed today. During the next 30 minutes, I want each group to reach a consensus about the following question: How would you develop a new shopping center in this community?

- The U.S. Supreme Court has ruled that our state must develop a plan that reveals a more equitable distribution of funding to finance public education for students in our elementary and secondary schools. How would you propose to solve the problem?

Probing questions. One of the key strategies for engaging students in discussions is to use probing questions — "Why?" When you have raised a question and the student has given you a "Yes" or "No" or simplistic response, follow up with "Why?" This forces the student to go beyond surface responses to your questions, to reveal thought processes, knowledge bases, and sources of information, and to develop an ability to think above the recall and comprehension levels.

Integrating cooperative learning and critical thinking

An instructor could organize the class into small groups and then assign problems to the groups so that they use a technique that Cross and Angelo (1988) call "Documented Problem-Set Solutions." The purpose of the technique is to have group members actually document in writing the steps they take in solving their problems, and to share their steps with their classmates at the close of the activity, so that you can assess their problem-solving methods.

Students or groups could also trade papers and analyze each other's steps or each group's steps in solving the problems. Cross and Angelo believe that the technique can be used in areas as diverse as accounting, algebra, calculus, statistics, law, organic chemistry, grammar, music, and computer programming. You develop an initial set of problems for the groups to solve, then use a variety of questions throughout the entire problem-solving experience, thus integrating cooperative learning, critical thinking, and the use of questions.

Using a Systematic Instruction Model (SIM)

During the late 1970s, when I reviewed the literature about advance organizers, behavioral objectives, cues, positive reinforcement, and corrective feedback, I began to explore with a model for systematically instructing students during classroom sessions. I shared the model with graduate students in my "College Teaching" course. Next, I developed it as a module entitled "Alternatives to the Lecture: Expository Teaching, Mastery Learning, and Individualizing Instruction" and included it among several modules that I copyrighted in 1981 (Library of Congress, Copyright Txu 66509).

I encouraged graduate students to conduct research studies in the use of the Systematic Instruction Model. Some of my colleagues and I have used the model in conducting several studies of our own, which have been published in national journals (Vietor, Brubaker, Milford, and Johnson, 1985; Johnson, 1987a; Milford, Brubaker, and Johnson, 1991; Johnson, Burlbaw, and Willson, 1994).

In its present form, the Systematic Instruction Model (SIM) consists of the following steps (see Figure 5.1):

- The instructor begins the lesson with an advance organizer. This is a statement in writing or made verbally that tells the students what the lesson is about, but does not provide specifics.

  An advance organizer in writing might consist of a short article about the U.S. Civil War, but the article would not deal with the specifics that the instructor will use in a classroom presentation.

  A verbal advance organizer might consist of as few words as "We have been reading articles about the Civil War. Today I want to discuss two great generals, Robert E. Lee and U.S. Grant."

  Such advance organizers help the students establish a mind set for what is about to take place. After referencing Ausubel's early work with advance organizers, Snapp and Glover (1990) describe an experiment involving undergraduate college students and report that those "who read and paraphrased an advance organizer prior to reading an essay and answering adjunct questions over the essay correctly answered a significantly greater number of questions than did students not encountering the advance organizer" (p. 269).

- Next, the instructor presents — in writing or verbally — the behavioral objectives for the lesson.

  An example of a behavioral objective might be as follows: "After discussing the backgrounds and experiences of Robert E. Lee and U. S. Grant, the students will identify three potential reasons why each general became famous following the Civil War." This specificity tells the students exactly what the instructor expects of them and enhances the instructor's teaching because it requires more organization and planning in advance of the lesson.

- Next, the instructor begins what I have labeled "the interaction cycle." The interaction cycle has five more steps:

1. The instructor provides directions and gives cues to the students. For example, "Be sure to record the following in your notes because you will have to recall them when you take the final examination in the course." Such a statement highlights the critical importance of what the instructor is about to present.

2. The instructor presents information, concepts, and/or generalizations for about five to ten minutes. Using the above as a reference point, the instructor might talk about some characteristics of Robert E. Lee. The instructor attempts to restrict his or her talking because many students have short attention spans unless there is a change of pace or an activity is inserted during the lesson.

3. The instructor interjects questions about the content just presented to the students. This triggers "active interaction" among the students and the instructor.

4. The instructor either provides positive reinforcement ("That's a great response to my question!") or indirectly corrects the student ("Do the remainder of the students in the class agree with the response? Why not?").

5. The "interaction cycle" is repeated throughout the remainder of the lesson:

   - Cue the students

   - Present content

   - Ask questions about the content presented

   - Provide either positive reinforcement or corrective feedback

   - Repeat the cycle

You may want to try SIM during one of your lessons to see if the students appear to make better progress, and to discover if you like using SIM.

Figure 5.1 Systematic Instruction Model (SIM)

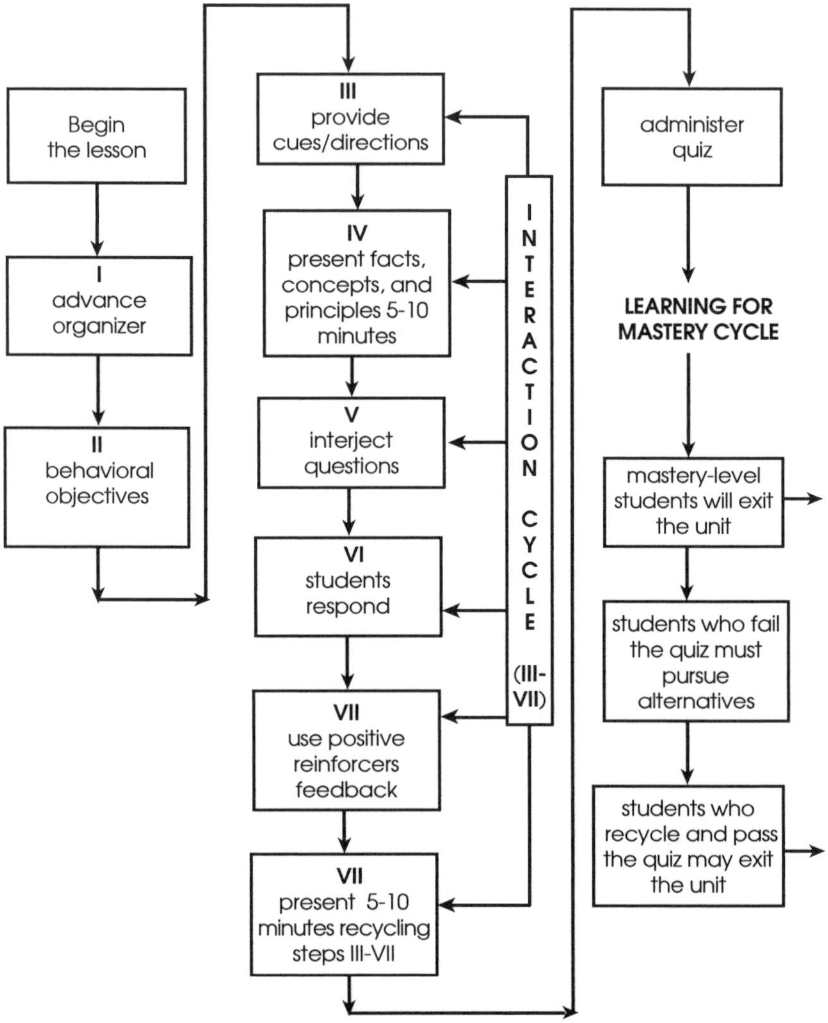

Begin the lesson

I advance organizer

II behavioral objectives

III provide cues/directions

IV present facts, concepts, and principles 5-10 minutes

V interject questions

VI students respond

VII use positive reinforcers feedback

VII present 5-10 minutes recycling steps III-VII

INTERACTION CYCLE (III-VII)

administer quiz

LEARNING FOR MASTERY CYCLE

mastery-level students will exit the unit

students who fail the quiz must pursue alternatives

students who recycle and pass the quiz may exit the unit

Using the Cognitive Interaction Analysis System (CIAS) to Improve Discussions

I have developed a Cognitive Interaction Analysis System (CIAS) to improve discussions (Johnson, 1987b). If we accept the idea that teaching and learning involve at least to some extent reciprocal, interdependent communication between two or more people (teacher and learners), we can study one set of variables — verbal interactions — and help you analyze this phase of your teaching as well as your students' learning.

When students are encouraged to interact with each other in an orderly manner, thinking occurs because one student's contribution builds upon another student's contribution under the guidance of the instructor.

Interaction analysis involves coding classroom verbal statements, organizing the coded data, displaying the data in a useful way, and inferring conclusions about the teaching and learning that took place during a lesson.

I started by developing a set of 10 categories for all of the verbal statements that take place in college classrooms. Next, I developed descriptions of the categories and examples of each category, as well as a set of rules to guide the observers, and then assigned numerals to each of the 10 categories.

Users of the system are trained to record the classroom interaction, i.e., they listen to a number of audiotaped class segments until they memorize the categories and the numeral for each category, then write down the numeral that identifies each verbal interaction. The data are converted to a matrix format that enables the instructor to interpret the flow of the verbal interaction that took place in the classroom. This procedure is very similar to one developed by Flanders (1970, p. 28-29).

I believe that if you train yourself to use interaction analysis you will improve your verbal behavior in the classroom. In fact, my studies have supported my contention. Research studies have revealed significant changes in the verbal behavior of instructors, accompanied by increased student learning, when instructors used interaction analysis (Johnson, 1976b; Johnson, 1987a; Johnson, 1987b; Vietor, Brubaker, Milford, and Johnson, 1985).

Expository Teaching (ET) is also enhanced when you learn an interaction analysis system. ET involves selecting, organizing, translating, and presenting content in a flexible manner during a supervised unit of study when instructor-student and student-student interactions are encouraged throughout the delivery of the subject matter.

College instructors who were trained in interaction analysis found the training useful in their teaching (Johnson, 1976b). Interaction analysis has made instructors more aware of inconsistencies between instructional goals and cognitive behavior (Vietor, Brubaker, Milford and Johnson, 1985).

Perhaps I should briefly mention the work of Bloom (1976), since his research influenced me to include his findings within four of the 10 categories. Bloom identified four major elements related to Quality of Instruction:

- Cues provided by the instructor
- Participation by the students
- Reinforcement techniques used by the instructor
- Feedback/correctives provided by the instructor

The CIAS has 10 categories. The first seven categories represent teacher talk, while two are for student talk and one is for silent pauses of three or more seconds.

Category 1: Instructor accepts student attitudes

Identify as 1 non-threatening comments by the instructor that express acceptance of students' attitudes — either negative or positive.

An instructor may support positive attitudes as follows: "All of you appear to be very confident about tomorrow's quiz, and I'm sure you will do well." An example of accepting negative attitudes would be: "You appear to be upset about the grades." Instead of attacking or criticizing a student who expresses a negative feeling, the instructor communicates that he or she recognizes the negative attitude. This approach prevents embarrassing situations.

Jokes and humorous stories told by the instructor are also recorded as Category 1.

Category 1 comments are quite rare in college classrooms. My students compiled over 39,000 tallies of verbal interaction from 48 classrooms, and only one-tenth of 1% of the tallies fell into Category 1.

Perhaps instructors haven't paid enough attention to the power of this type of verbal behavior. They may not have their antennae up for student input. This is a skill you should develop as a beginning instructor.

Category 2: Instructor uses positive reinforcement

Identify as 2 any instructor statement that communicates a definite value judgment, indicating that he or she really likes what the student said or did. For example: "Excellent! That's a great suggestion!"

Almost every theorist has supported reinforcement as facilitating learning (Bergan and Dunn, 1976, p. 212). Responses followed by rewards strengthen learning (Bugelski, 1971, p. 57-58). "Learning takes place only when the act that is performed is reinforced" (Symonds, 1968, p. 11). Powerful extrinsic reinforcers, such as verbal praise by the instructor, can be a valuable tool for learning.

One caution: don't overuse positive statements. They must be appropriate reactions. In fact, once learning is progressing well within a unit of study, it may be advisable to reduce or omit reinforcers from time to time (Bugelski, 1971, p. 96).

Keep in mind that an instructor's statement is categorized as a positive reinforcer only if his or her voice communicates enthusiasm and expresses that he or she really likes the student's response or action. If this is not clearly signaled, the statement is probably a Category 3.

Category 3: Instructor uses corrections or provides feedback

These statements are non-punitive and non-threatening, such as "No" or "Yes" or "That's correct." If the instructor merely repeats a student's response so that all students know that it was correct or acceptable, use Category 3, as depicted in the following:

Student: "Abe Lincoln."

Instructor: "Abe Lincoln." [Category 3] or "Yes, John, that is the correct answer." [Category 3]

Category 3 is used when the instructor's voice does not communicate a value judgment of really liking the student's response. Compare the following:

Student: "Abe Lincoln."

Instructor: "Abe Lincoln!" [Category 2] or "Yes, that's great!" [Category 2].

Rosenshine (1976) reviewed research studies that involved corrective feedback. He reports (p. 361):

> 19 of the 20 correlations were positive, and 13 were significant. This positive correlation held regardless of the type of feedback, that is, even for negative feedback. ... Such results suggest that the topic of feedback ... is more important than the type of feedback.

Symonds (1968) references the works of Edward Thorndike and B.F. Skinner, indicating that the use of the word "wrong" has no negative impact on learning if the teacher's tone isn't harsh (p. 29). He notes that an experiment by Elizabeth Bergne Hurlock revealed that praise was three to four times superior to reproof, but Symonds also believes that both forms serve as incentives in learning (p. 31). He thinks that a very mild punishment doesn't actually hurt the student, and that any anxiety would hardly be recognizable, although it would provide a signal to the learner to guide behavior and responses (p. 31).

We don't want students to leave our classrooms with wrong understandings. Therefore, I think we need to employ more corrections and provide more feedback during class time.

Category 4: Instructor asks questions

Identify as 4 any question, including rhetorical questions and cases in which the instructor rephrases a student's comment in the form of a question:

Student: "It's a desolate area and would deter growth potential."

Instructor: "Are you saying that the location is removed from modes of transportation?" (Category 4)

The instructor's questions are important to student learning. Studies have revealed positive and significant correlations between instructors' questions and students' achievement, when direct questions focus on academics.

We ask questions to invite students to participate and contribute their ideas, opinions, or knowledge. Gall and Gall (1976) indicate that the instructor's questions promoted learning even for students who just listened to the discussion while engaging in convergent learning (p. 210).

Responses to the instructor's questions can provide opportunities for feedback, for both students and instructors. Some teachers ask questions at the beginning of a class to determine the progress the students are making, so responses serve as information that the instructor can use to move the students toward desired objectives (Shavelson, 1976, p. 412).

Category 5: Instructor lectures

Identify as 5 instructor talk that communicates facts, expresses ideas, or provides illustrations. Category 5 usually has the highest frequency of tallies of all 10 categories. Of the 39,000 tallies recorded in various classrooms, my students identified almost two-thirds as Category 5; in some disciplines, more than 70% of the tallies were recorded as Category 5. Lecture is the primary mode of presenting basic subject matter; therefore, the predominance of Category 5 tallies should come as no surprise.

Category 6: Instructor gives cues or directions

Identify as 6 words that signal importance — "This is important to remember; record it in your notebooks" — and statements that require the students to do something — "Mary, give me the answer to problem 43" or "Look at the five genres of literature listed on the blackboard. Keep them in mind throughout the lesson." Cues or directions may appear anytime, interspersed throughout the lesson.

Many descriptions of cues create problems for people who are recording interaction analysis; they struggle with beginning and ending parts of statements and find overlap with other categories of interaction if the definition of a cue is restrictive.

Bloom (1976, p. 115) provides the following help:

Cues may be relatively simple, such as a sound or word to be related to a particular object, event, or activity; the relating of a particular signal; the demonstration of a sequence of physical activity; or the directions for a complex set of cognitive processes.

For CIAS, cues and directions are verbal signals to pay attention to what is about to follow or to react to something. I combine directions and cues because giving directions is related to cueing. Cues gain the attention of the listener and highlight events. After highlighting or giving procedural directions (Category 6), instructors usually return to presenting more information to the students (Category 5).

Category 7: Instructor criticizes students

Identify as 7 any negative, punitive comments, strong criticism, and blame — "Ridiculous" or "That's silly" or "Don't interrupt me when I'm giving my lectures."

Although CIAS attaches no rating or value scale to each category, Category 7 should be avoided as much as possible. Blame or a feeling of failure inflicts a kind of pain. Many students can describe the feeling of helplessness that grabbed them when an instructor rendered an intensive verbal attack. Instead of responding with thoughtful contributions, they froze or repeated their original, erroneous answers.

Smith (1971) reviews several studies and reports (p. 50-51):

The stronger forms of criticism had a higher negative correlation with achievement than the milder form. Thus, teachers who use extreme amounts of forms of criticism usually have classes which achieve less in most subject areas.

Category 8: Cognitive student talk

Identify as 8 student talk that is oriented around subject matter:

- Recalling facts
- Responding to instructor questions or directions with subject matter responses or questions
- Expressing opinions or ideas about topics under study
- Analyzing, synthesizing, or evaluating

Cognitive student talk can be viewed as a form of participation and/or recitation. Students are responding when they talk, and they are learning.

Various studies on recitation support this viewpoint (Bloom, 1976; Symonds, 1968).

Category 9: Non-cognitive student talk

Identify as 9 student talk that is not related to subject matter — "Can we leave now?" or "Can we take a break?" or "I went to the basketball game last night" or "Is the quiz tomorrow instead of Friday?"

Category 9 accounts for probably less than 1% of the total tallies recorded in most classrooms.

Category 0: Silence

Identify as 0 pauses of three full seconds or longer when there is no verbal communication or when communication can't be understood. Silence occurs when students are reflecting or reading silently, or when the instructor is rearranging some equipment for a demonstration or writing on the board silently.

In order for a Category 0 to be recorded, the silence must be a full three seconds or more. (This is the only category of CIAS where each tally must be a full three seconds before it can be recorded.) We use a 0 rather than 10 because it is easier and quicker to write, and more convenient when using the computer program to produce CIAS printouts.

All 10 categories of CIAS are summarized in Figure 6.1 on the next page.

Procedures for recording CIAS

Once the observer (that's you if you're replaying an audiotape of your lesson) feels comfortable and notes that the lesson is under way, he or she records the time, writes down a 0 to begin, and at the close of each three seconds decides which category best represents the interaction that took place during that three-second period. The observer writes the category numbers in sequence, one by one, until the lesson is completed. The end is marked as a 0. It is important to record a 0 to begin the lesson and a 0 at the end of the lesson. These two 0's, in contrast to 0's recorded during the lesson, are used to show the opening and the closing of the lesson.

You will probably feel overwhelmed during the first two or three hours of using CIAS. That's normal. I have trained thousands of people in interaction analysis, and every one experienced the same frustration during the first few hours of practice. But 99% became excellent recorders of interaction analysis. You, too, will develop the timing and expertise in recording interaction analysis every three seconds after you have

Figure 6.1 Cognitive Interaction Analysis System (CIAS) Categories

Silence Category (0)	
Category 0 — Silence	Three seconds or more of silence; pauses when no communication exists for three seconds or more; noisy confusion when it is not possible to decipher the talk, such as when students are noisy while rearranging the room for group activities.

Teacher Talk Categories (1-7)	
Category 1 — Accepting Student Attitudes	Comments that communicate a non-threatening acceptance of student attitudes, positive or negative, e.g., "You appear to be upset about this" or "I'm glad to see that all of you are happy about the results from last week's test."
Category 2 — Positive Reinforcement	Praising students; communicating a definite value judgment indicating that the instructor likes what the student said or did, e.g., "Excellent!" or "Very good!"
Category 3— Correction or Feedback	Includes negative statements that are nonpunitive and nonthreatening; saying "no" or "yes" or "that's correct" in a manner that provides feedback to students; repeating a student's response so that all students know that it was correct or acceptable.
Category 4 — Questions	Includes rhetorical questions; all questions raised by the teacher; calling on student by name if the student has raised his or her hand to respond to a question.
Category 5 — Lecture	Communicating facts, expressing ideas, giving examples, providing illustrations.
Category 6 — Cues or Directions	Words that signal importance: "This is important to remember!" or "These next four items may appear on your final exam." Directions for the students to follow, including procedural directions; calling a student's name with the purpose of directing him or her to respond.
Category 7 — Criticism	Negative, punitive comments; strong criticism; blaming students; saying "Ridiculous" or "That's silly" or "Don't interrupt me like that when I'm giving my lecture."

Student Talk Categories (8-9)	
Category 8 — Cognitive Student Talk	Talk by students that is subject-oriented: recalling facts; responding to instructor questions or directions with subject-matter responses or subject-matter questions; expressing opinions or ideas about topics under study; analyzing, synthesizing, evaluating; raising subject-matter questions.
Category 9 — Non-Cognitive Student Talk	Talk by students that is not related to subject matter: management comments — "Can we leave now?" or "Will we have the quiz tomorrow?" or "I went to the game Saturday and didn't have time to prepare my paper."

memorized the 10 categories, learned the ground rules, and practiced for a few hours. Hang in there! It is like any other skill: practice makes perfect.

Rules for recording CIAS

1. Do not record CIAS during the opening of the class session, when the instructor is dealing with management tasks instead of cognitive aspects of the lesson (e.g., checking attendance, collecting assignments, returning tests).

2. Begin to record CIAS when the instructor and/or students engage in cognitive aspects of the lesson. Students can initiate the interaction; for example, a student might ask, "Last time you talked about ... . What did you mean?"

3. Record the numeral representing the interaction category once every three seconds.

4. If more than one category of interaction is in evidence during a three-second period, record each category.

5. Except when beginning and ending a lesson, record a 0 only when there is a total of three seconds of silence, confusion, or unrecordable noise.

6. Do not use the CIAS if the class views a film, listens to a lengthy audiotape, or spends the class time in silent reading. Merely record the time and write a comment describing the situation. Wait until the instructor is again engaged in cognitive verbal interaction.

7. When in doubt, record the category that is congruent with the predominant mood. For example, if the situation isn't a clear Category 2 or Category 3, think about the previous statements. If the instructor has consistently accepted student responses by repeating or rewording them instead of enthusiastically praising them, record a 3.

8. If there are very long periods of time when communication is undecipherable, or when there's chaos, stop recording 0's and write a comment and the time. When the class settles and cognitive interaction resumes, note the time and begin recording again.

9. When the instructor is interacting with several students during a planned cognitive lesson and some students are chatting among themselves, record CIAS for the verbal interaction between the instructor and the students and ignore the chatting. If the class

becomes disruptive, however, and it is apparent that the instructor is disorganized, stop recording, note the time, and write a comment.

Here is an example of the first and last 15 seconds of a lesson:

9:03 a.m.

0 (to mark the start of the recording of interaction analysis; this 0 is not included as part of the first 15 seconds of verbal interaction)

5

5

0

5

5

... (end of first 15 seconds of lesson)

4

8

8

0

6

0 (to mark the end of the last 15 seconds of the lesson; this 0 is not included as part of the last 15 seconds of verbal interaction)

Limitations

By now you have recognized some of the limitations of CIAS. Good! CIAS doesn't provide data about management techniques, isn't appropriate for independent study settings, and doesn't indicate the type of questions the instructor asks.

Matrices

Now that you've sequentially recorded the categories, how do you interpret your data?

Transfer the numerals to a 10x10 matrix, either manually or by computer. (I prefer the computer program since it is so much easier and quicker.)

Pair each numeral with the numeral following. For example, for the sequence 0 3 6 4 8, we have the following pairs: 0-3, 3-6, 6-4, 4-8. The first numeral of each pair designates the *row*, while the second numeral of the pair designates the *column*. The tally (/) is marked (placed) on the matrix where the row and column intersect; e.g., a tally in the 3-6 cell means a 3 was followed by a 6. Then the second numeral of the previous tally is paired with the next numeral recorded, to form the new pair:

3

(first pair: 3-6)

6

(second pair: 6-4)

4

(third pair: 4-8)

8

Look at Figure 6.2. The above three pairs are represented by a tally mark in row 3 - column 6, a tally mark in row 6 - column 4, and a tally mark in row 4 - column 8.

The actual data will be transposed into tallies appearing within the 100 cells of the 10x10 matrix. The computer program totals the tallies in each

Figure 6.2 Response Matrix

Category	0	1	2	3	4	5	6	7	8	9
0										
1										
2										
3							/			
4									/	
5										
6					/					
7										
8										
9										

cell; if you are doing this manually, you have to count your tallies in each cell after completing the matrix.

Analysis

You are now ready to analyze the completed matrix. Look for cells with heavy concentrations of tallies. Those represent the CIAS categories most used during the lesson.

The shaded areas in Figure 6.3 show a pattern in which the instructor asks a question, the student responds to the question, and the instructor provides corrective/feedback.

The shaded areas in Figure 6.4 show a pattern in which the instructor asks a question, the student responds to the question, and the instructor provides reinforcement.

If you want to know the kind of categories that *preceded* harsh criticism by the instructor, you would look down the 7 column (excluding the 7-7 cell). If one or more tallies appear in the 6-7 cell, for example, you know that cues/directions preceded harsh criticism. If one or more tallies appear in the 10-7 cell, you know that silence preceded the harsh criticism. You exclude the 7-7 cell because it indicates only the use of criticism for more than three consecutive seconds, and not which category preceded or followed the 7's.

Figure 6.3 Instructor-provided corrective feedback matrix

Category	0	1	2	3	4	5	6	7	8	9
0										
1										
2										
3										
4										
5										
6										
7										
8										
9										

Figure 6.4 Instructor provided reinforcement matrix

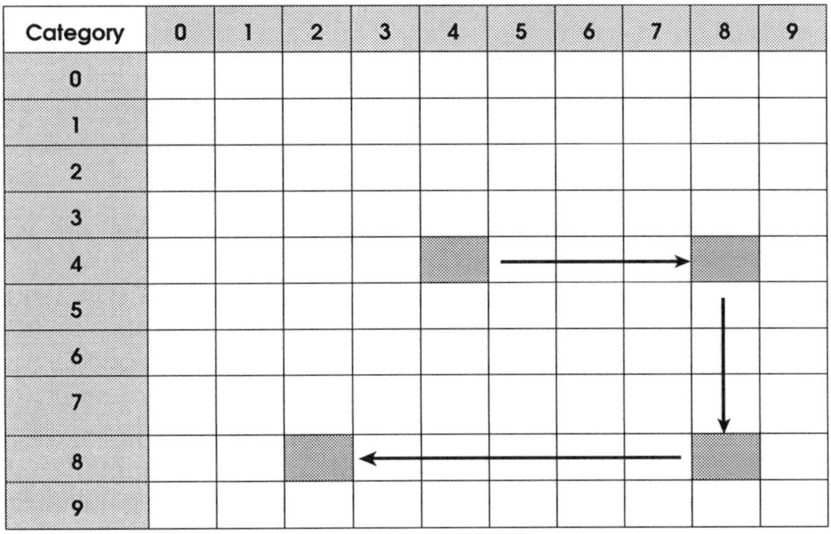

Category	0	1	2	3	4	5	6	7	8	9
0										
1										
2										
3										
4										
5										
6										
7										
8										
9										

Conversely, if you want to know the kind of categories that *followed* an instructor's question, you would look along the 4 row (excluding the 4-4 cell). If several tallies appear in the 4-8 cell, for example, you know the number of times students responded immediately to the instructor's questions.

Figure 6.5 Matrix of Pairs (Example)

Category	0	1	2	3	4	5	6	7	8	9
0	3	0	0	0	5	6	3	0	5	0
1	0	6	0	0	2	1	1	0	1	0
2	0	0	2	0	8	5	2	0	1	0
3	1	1	7	15	23	13	6	0	2	0
4	10	2	0	1	92	5	5	0	58	0
5	1	0	2	3	22	94	7	0	1	0
6	7	0	1	0	12	4	73	0	0	0
7	0	0	0	0	0	0	0	0	0	0
8	0	2	6	49	9	2	0	0	33	0
9	0	0	0	0	0	0	0	0	0	0
SUM	22	11	18	68	173	130	97	0	101	0

Frequencies, Ratios, and Percentages

Look at Figure 6.5. The matrix displays the data collected by one observer using CIAS during an English class. The lesson was about 31 minutes long. One tally recorded every three seconds yields (one tally every three seconds yields 20 tallies per minute, which in turn yields 620 tallies in 31 minutes).

The following formulas allow you to interpret the matrix in Figure 6.5:

1. SC (silence) indicates the percentage of the total time devoted to silence (each three seconds of silence). It is calculated by taking the total number of tallies in either row 0 or column 0 (they have the same total) and dividing by the total number of all tallies, which in this case is 620.

2. TT (teacher talk) indicates the percentage of the total time the instructor talked. It is calculated by taking the sum of Categories 1 + 2 + 3 + 4 + 5 + 6 + 7 (in either their rows or their columns) which, again, are equal, and dividing by the total number of tallies, 620.

3. PT (pupil talk) indicates the percentage of the total time the students talked. It is calculated by taking the sum of Categories 8 + 9 (in either their rows or their columns) and dividing by the total number of tallies, 620.

4. PTC (pupil talk cognitive) indicates the amount of total student talk that involved cognitive aspects of the lesson. It is calculated by taking the sum of Category 8 (in either row 8 or column 8) and dividing by the total number of tallies for Categories 8 + 9 (in either their rows or their columns).

5. PSSR (total amount of student talk in the same category for more than three seconds, but combining these totals for Categories 8 and 9) is calculated by taking all the tallies in the 8-8 cell plus all the tallies in the 9-9 cell and dividing by the total number of tallies for Categories 8 + 9 (in either their rows or their columns).

6. TSSR (total number of teacher talk in the same category for more than three seconds) is calculated by taking all the tallies in cells 1-1, 2-2, 3-3, 4-4, 5-5, 6-6, and 7-7 and dividing by the total number of tallies for Categories 1 + 2 + 3 + 4 + 5 + 6 + 7 (in either their rows or their columns).

7. Q (questions) is a fairly accurate inference about the total number of different times the instructor asks questions. Q is calculated by taking the sum of Category 4 (in either the Category 4 row or the Category 4 column) and subtracting the tallies in the 4-4 cell.

8. CF (corrective/feedback) is a fairly accurate inference about the total number of different times the instructor provides corrective/feedback to student talk. CF is calculated by taking the sum of Category 3 in either the Category 3 row or the Category 3 column and subtracting the tallies in the 3-3 cell.

9. R (positive reinforcement) is a fairly accurate inference about the total number of times students receive positive reinforcement from the instructor. R is calculated by taking the sum of Category 2 (in either the Category 2 row or the Category 2 column) and subtracting the tallies in the 2-2 cell.

You can now analyze the matrix located in Figure 6.5.

- Silence accounted for approximately 4% of the total time.

  SC = 22 (tallies in either row 0 or column 0) ÷ 620 (total tallies) = 3.56%.

- What percentage of the total time was devoted to instructor talk? About 80%.

  TT = 497 (tallies in Categories 1-7) ÷ 620 (total tallies) = 80.16%.

- What percentage of the total time was devoted to student talk? About 16%.

  PT = 101 (tallies in Categories 8 and 9) ÷ 620 (total tallies) = 16.29%.

We can also discover the number of times the instructor asked questions, the number of times the instructor provided corrective/feedback, and the number of times the instructor gave positive reinforcement.

- How many questions did the instructor ask? 81.

  Q = 173 (tallies in Category 4) - 92 (tallies in the 4-4 cell) = 81.

  It seems fair to conclude that the instructor used a Socratic approach during the lesson.

- How many times did the instructor make corrections or provide feedback to the students? 53.

  CF = 68 (tallies in Category 3) - 15 (tallies in the 3-3 cell) = 53.

  I think this was advisable when dealing with content new to the students. The Category 3 tallies were prompted by the large number of instructor questions followed by student responses, for which the instructor provided corrective/feedback.

- How often did the instructor use positive reinforcement? 16 times.

Figure 6.6 Percentages for Observations (Example)

Category	0	1	2	3	4	5	6	7	8	9
0	0.5	0.0	0.0	0.0	0.8	1.0	0.5	0.0	0.8	0.0
1	0.0	1.0	0.0	0.0	0.3	0.2	0.2	0.0	0.2	0.0
2	0.0	0.0	0.3	0.0	1.3	0.8	0.3	0.0	0.2	0.0
3	0.2	0.2	1.1	2.4	3.7	2.1	1.0	0.0	0.3	0.0
4	1.6	0.3	0.0	0.2	14.8	0.8	0.8	0.0	9.4	0.0
5	0.2	0.0	0.3	0.5	3.5	15.2	1.1	0.0	0.2	0.0
6	1.1	0.0	0.2	0.0	1.9	0.6	11.8	0.0	0.0	0.0
7	0.0	0.0	0.0	0.0	0.0	0.0	0.0	0.0	0.0	0.0
8	0.0	0.3	1.0	7.9	1.5	0.3	0.0	0.0	5.3	0.0
9	0.0	0.0	0.0	0.0	0.0	0.0	0.0	0.0	0.0	0.0
SUM	3.6	1.8	2.9	11.0	27.8	21.0	15.7	0.0	16.4	0.0

R = 18 (tallies in Category 2) - 2 (tallies in the 2-2 cell) = 16.

Since the content was new to the students, the instructor was wise to provide positive reinforcement for correct answers. This would help to build the confidence of the students as they explored the new content.

- All of the student talk was cognitive.

PTC = 101 (tallies in Category 8) ÷ 101 (total tallies in Category 8 + Category 9) = 100%.

- About a third of the talk by students lasted three seconds or more in any one category.

PSSR = 33 (tallies in 8-8 cell and 9-9 cell) ÷ 101 (total tallies in Category 8 + Category 9) = 32.67%.

This means that most of the students responses were short, perhaps only a few words (smaller number of tallies in 8-8 cell compared with total number of tallies in Category 8).

- A little over half of the instructor's talk lasted more than three seconds.

TSSR = 282 (total tallies in seven cells: 6 in 1-1, 2 in 2-2, 15 in 3-3, 92 in 4-4, 94 in 5-5, 73 in 6-6, 0 in 7-7) ÷ 497 (total tallies in Categories 1-7) = 56.74%.

Since most college classes reveal a much higher TSSR, and because of our analysis of other key categories dealing with

Figure 6.7 Final Results (Example)

Q = 81	CF = 53	R = 16
SC = 3.55%	TT = 80.16%	PT = 16.29%
PTC = 100.00%	PSSR = 32.67%	TSSR = 56.74%

cues, questions, corrective feedback, and student cognitive talk, we can infer that the instructor was engaging the students in relatively substantial interaction when compared with most other college classes.

The instructor appears to have been in control of the lesson, an inference drawn from the total number of tallies in steady-state cells (PSSR, TSSR). The climate of the classroom appeared to encourage student participation (tallies in Categories 1 and 2 versus zero tallies in Category 7). This was obviously a cognitive-oriented lesson (large number of tallies in Categories 3, 4, 5, 6, and 8).

Practice makes proficient

You need to practice with CIAS by replaying an audiotape of one of your lessons. If another instructor is interested in CIAS training, ask him or her

Figure 6.8 Original Input Data (Example)

0555544444	4843483483	4484484834	8483541144	8334883444
8118348883	3554441155	543334006	2448488883	4489444448
3444448336	4444454488	832255556	6666648483	5544834834
8483666644	8348348348	3555544448	4883488324	8324836644
4440444828	3444583348	3244888883	2555555555	6666555554
4882555555	6666660483	3344883554	0835354008	8255555260
0555483354	8354885524	8333455644	4448833388	8324444482
2536660555	5555555555	5555483835	4444488834	4448324455
4483364404	4466666655	5555555605	5445554088	8833554665
5550556555	4040554483	5555555555	5554444444	8266644440
8834466666	6666666606	6644883530	4408555555	5666444444
484444488	1144844883	6666644888	8311166666	6666666666
6666064666	6664446666	0		

to practice with you so that you can take turns discussing each other's recorded classroom data. If the two of you disagree, discuss why and attempt to reach a consensus. This also builds a nice support group that can "talk about teaching." You are making excellent progress when other observers and you agree 65% or more of the time, but don't expect to reach such a lofty level in the first few hours of training.

After you have become proficient in the use of CIAS, you may want to conduct research using the system. For research purposes, it would be best if observers practice until they reach an agreement level of 85% or greater.

Practice lesson

A short lesson of about 10 minutes is located in the Appendix. The goal of the lesson is to discuss various types of energy, while focusing on nuclear energy. The specific objective is to have the students identify at least four sources of energy, differentiate between fission and fusion, and identify one favorable aspect and one unfavorable aspect of fission and of fusion.

The lesson is a real lesson taught to real students, and it demonstrates how an instructor can do the following within 10 minutes:

- State a generic goal for the lesson in an opening statement
- State a behavioral objective for the lesson
- Present more than 15 facts and two major concepts
- Ask 13 questions
- Bring closure to this segment of the lesson

Going Beyond
Lectures and Discussions

Many instructors teach primarily or even solely through lectures and discussions. They limit themselves and their students unnecessarily. Your course objectives may well take you beyond lectures and discussions. This chapter will cover some of those other ways of facilitating learning — case studies, simulations, field trips, Keller Plan, and laboratory method.

Case studies

Case studies are widely used in law and business courses. They are appropriate for other disciplines when the lesson objectives include analyzing, synthesizing, and judging. When using case studies, the instructor provides the students with ample background information and data about a hypothetical situation so they can attack a problem and apply basic concepts and principles.

A case is a scaled-down replication of a real experience or series of events, with ample problems or issues to generate a good discussion. You might interview real people about normal, everyday happenings that include realistic confrontations, ambiguities, problems, issues, crises, and controversies. Then provide the students with materials that set up specific situations and problems, followed by a series of questions.

Christensen and Hansen (1987, p. 4) recommend the case method approach for four reasons:

1. Discussion techniques, like the case study method, may be the best way to attain course objectives that involve higher cognitive skills and affective development.

2. Instructors can better analyze their ability to lead discussions by using cases. (This would be a good reason to use CIAS with an audiotape of one of your case study sessions — to analyze your ability to handle discussions.)

3. The case method approach is more relevant than many other strategies, since it brings the students closer to reality.

4. The case method approach is a scholarly undertaking that "offers opportunities for systematic inquiry and rigorous reasoning."

Learned (1987) offers several suggestions from students who have participated in case studies:

- Establish a clear set of objectives for the case study.
- Provide leadership during discussions: intercede if the students stray off the track and raise some key questions to help them refocus their efforts.
- Keep the students from continually repeating lessons already learned.
- Build on any important items that emerge as sidelines during the discussions. (These are "teachable moments": if they're relevant, use them.)
- Insist that students declare their positions.
- Stress attendance and participation.
- Cue the students when they're moving in the appropriate direction, with a comment such as "That's an interesting proposal, Jean."
- Use the opening minutes to solicit a list of key topics to be discussed.
- Encourage and guide, but refrain from actively participating.
- Give a critique in the middle and at the end of a class period.

Hansen (1987) wisely suggests that instructors encourage class participation and communication by not providing answers. If a student asks a question, turn it back to the class or choose another student to respond.

Hansen (p. 59) offers another suggestion:

> To help sustain a smooth pace and further encourage the group to work together, you might call on two or three students at once and ask them to collaborate on some particularly elusive point of discussion for the rest of the class.

What is the instructor's role when using the case study method? Christensen and Hansen (1987) suggest that the emphasis should be on encouraging learning instead of stressing teaching. They propose that the instructor move away from the "status of a center-stage, intellectually superior authority figure." The instructor must teach the skills of "observation, listening, communication, and decision-making" by actually modeling such practices (pp. 31-32).

How does the instructor prepare for day-to-day class sessions with case studies? Christensen and Hansen (pp. 38-39) suggest the following steps:

1. Review your objectives for the class session (usually problem-solving objectives).

2. Prepare materials you will distribute for students to read.

3. Consider critical issues and topics yet to be covered.

4. Summarize notes following each class session, and make a general review of previous class sessions.

5. Analyze the simulated industry, business, or organization situation, suggest possible conclusions to problems, and then develop a set of appropriate recommendations.

6. Hypothesize how the discussion of the case will progress.

7. Consider the background and experiences of each student's strengths and limitations.

8. Consider your attitude about the case, in order to prevent your biases from emerging and distorting the learning process.

9. Attempt to develop opening comments and closing summaries.

One of the major, substantive lessons learned from the experiences of the faculty associated with developing instructional case studies for the Harvard Business School was that instructors can learn a lot about their teaching if they willingly work together to analyze what happened while teaching cases.

Zeakes (1989) describes an interesting approach to the use of case studies. He has students create their own case studies about parasitic conditions (including all of the symptoms, pathology, epidemiology, and diagnosis), with the exception of the specific parasite being described. The other students try to figure out which parasite the "case study" is describing.

Simulations

Simulations are closely allied to case studies. They are particularly useful when lesson objectives include recognition of and appreciation for the values and attitudes of other groups and cultures.

To set up a simulation, obtain as much information as possible about the group or culture to be studied, then have students actually play the roles of people from that group or culture. Set the stage for the activity by establishing ground rules, providing materials, and selecting players.

There are important advantages to using a simulation strategy:

- It can help students gain insights into their real feelings about situations, events, people, and cultures.
- It can be fun; students are positive in their feelings about the use of simulation strategies.
- It can motivate students to pursue information that might otherwise be of little interest to them.
- It can unleash creativity.
- It encourages spontaneity.
- It generally captures information, attitudes, and feelings in such a way that they are moved to long-term memory — a much stronger outcome than through passive learning strategies.
- It provides opportunities for students to try behaviors different from those they normally display.
- Students can better appreciate the attitudes of others: they can observe the behaviors of other students, listen to their suggestions, and build a respect for the viewpoints expressed by others.

There are some caveats:

- It requires very little student preparation, although you should have a solid set of objectives in mind before engaging the students in a simulation.
- Simulation can be very time-consuming. It wouldn't be appropriate if the course objectives are strongly oriented to covering a multitude of facts.
- Some students may not want to express themselves during simulations; if their self-esteem or self-confidence is low, they might find the experience threatening.
- Some students give simulation very little credence. One way to overcome this negative reaction is to invite a top management administrator (vice president, chief executive officer, manager) from business, industry, or education to visit your class and talk with your students about the benefits of simulation.

- Instructors need experience in using the strategy; you would be better prepared to use it if you attended training sessions. The experience of actually going through simulations with role-playing prior to using the strategy in your classes would help you understand simulation procedures and build your confidence.

- Students may not have enough basic knowledge about the culture or people to make meaningful contributions.

- There is always the danger of overly aggressive students dominating the scenario; some may make fun of those who play the roles. You can reduce these risks by orienting the students to the proper behavior you expect during simulation and role-playing.

What are some suggestions for first-time users of simulations?

- Prepare carefully; determine your objectives for the lesson — and keep them in mind.

- Take time to discuss the strategy with the students prior to their first experience with role-playing and simulation.

- Be sure to explain to the students how the activity relates to the objectives for the lesson and the course.

- Develop a wholesome classroom climate prior to using this strategy; I wait several weeks into my courses before I use simulation and role-playing.

- Try to list the questions that you hope the students will raise when they discuss the simulation; interject those that are not raised.

- Involve as many students as possible; you may want to have the same situation replayed by three groups of students.

Field trips

Sometimes you may prefer to take the students away from the campus to observe some phenomenon. Settings for field trips can be quite diverse: the court house, a local business, an art museum, an industrial site, a funeral parlor, an historical site, a farm or ranch, oil rig sites, a statesman's home, and so forth. Some trips are relatively simple; others can be quite ambitious.

First you need to decide if the field trip is the best way for the students to achieve the objective(s) for your proposed lesson.

If a field trip seems appropriate to your objective(s), you need to check your institution's faculty/student handbooks for answers to questions involving regulations about field trips. Among the usual preparations, you must:

- Clear everything with your immediate supervisor, usually the department chair
- Obtain permission slips
- Check on insurance
- Arrange for transportation
- Check out admission fees
- Ensure that either you or your students complete any official forms
- Prepare a handout for the students, indicating the purpose for the trip and your objectives, with a guide sheet, a map, departure/arrival times
- Note any reports to be filed after the trip

Next, you need to organize the field trip. A few guiding questions:

- When will it take place?
- Where will the students meet?
- How will the students travel to the site?
- How will money be collected?
- What arrangements must be made for any meals or overnight accommodations?
- What medical supplies may be needed?
- Whom should you contact in case of an emergency?

You still have some important tasks to complete prior to the field trip. You should personally go over the details with officials at the site — time, date, number of students, person to contact on arrival, etc. You should ask them about safety precautions and other restrictions they might have; for example, chemicals in a building may prevent access by students with contact lenses or the site may not be accessible to students with mobility handicaps.

One of the more important tasks is for you to take the field trip yourself before you take your students. You may discover that the trip takes longer than you estimated, so you should change your departure and return times. You may discover that a site is extremely hot or cold, so you should recommend that your students dress appropriately. You might discover a very interesting phenomenon at the site that students should note when they take the trip. You will also want to obtain the names of key personnel at the site, so you can add them to your handouts.

This preliminary visit also provides you with the opportunity to discuss with on-site personnel your purpose and objectives, as well as any items you'd like them to emphasize during the trip. It also allows you to better prepare your students, with confidence and authority.

Finally, you will want to consider the follow-up discussion and activities. Is the discussion best handled at the site, after departing from the site, or in the next class session? What is an appropriate and meaningful follow-up activity — oral reports, term papers, tests?

Many beginning instructors avoid field trips. Others dread the preparation and supervision. Some may question the "pedagogical justification" of such trips or simply feel uncomfortable about taking out a group of students as if they were a fourth-grade class. But if a field trip is appropriate to your objectives and, if you plan properly, it can be a most effective and satisfying activity.

Keller Plan

A Keller Plan divides the course into sections or units of study. Students refer to printed guides to help them progress through the course at their own pace; of course, the instructor or an assistant is available to help those students who need extra coaching or who have questions for which answers are not found in the guides and instructional materials. If the course is linear, you can establish unit tests and require students to reach an acceptable level of mastery prior to moving into the next unit of study. This means that some students may have to recycle through the materials and activities for a unit until they meet the predetermined "pass and progress" level, a kind of prerequisite before moving into the next unit.

A Keller Plan has five features that set it apart from traditional instructional strategies:

1. **The Keller Plan is mastery-oriented.** You have to determine in advance what you'll accept as "mastery" of the unit and how you'll measure the progress of the students.

2. **The Keller Plan emphasizes individual pacing.**

3. **The Keller Plan emphasizes self-tutoring.**

4. **The Keller Plan uses printed study guides to communicate information.** You need to invest a lot of time into developing these

study guides. The units should include introductions, objectives, cues, content, activities, directions, and self-scoring progress tests with feedback, so the students can tell if they are ready to take the unit test in an attempt to "pass and progress" into the next unit. I also recommend that you have a few students with diverse backgrounds read your study guides before you use them.

5. **The Keller Plan includes a few lectures by the instructor to motivate students.** You could post a notice on the bulletin board or use electronic mail to communicate specifics about your lectures.

For instructors interested in providing more opportunities for students to move at their own learning pace, the Keller Plan provides a means of addressing that concern. Two references of particular value are Watson (1986) and Rae (1993).

One fall term, I visited a college where a Keller Plan was in operation for students enrolled in Chemistry I and Chemistry II. I noted two students working in adjacent study carrels; one student was completing Chemistry II while the other was halfway through Chemistry I. However, the first student had been at the college only a few months, while the second student was completing her second year. The second student had been receiving "Incomplete" on her semester grade sheets because she was still struggling to learn the basic knowledge required to "pass and progress" through the units and into Chemistry II. The first student was extremely bright, entered with excellent prerequisites, sailed through Chemistry I, and was moving swiftly through Chemistry II. These two students illustrate the advantages of the Keller Plan.

Laboratory method

This method is widely used in scientific settings. The students can observe phenomena and the operation of substances. The laboratory method is appropriate for objectives that involve research methods, application, and observation skills. Students in chemistry can observe what happens when two specific chemicals are mixed. Art students always find that studio labs accompany their painting or sculpting activities. Architecture or civil engineering courses can provide laboratory opportunities for students to build small-scale models of buildings or bridges.

Laboratory instruction is one of the more practical alternatives to the lecture. It takes students away from the theoretical setting of the textbook and lecture, to confront them with problems to solve, experiments to conduct, demonstrations to observe, exercises to complete, short-term and long-term projects to pursue, or data to collect so they can interpret

First Steps to Excellence in College Teaching

and draw conclusions. The focus is on having students instruct themselves and each other.

Brown and Atkins (1987, p. 91) identify the following as worthwhile goals for laboratory teaching:

- Instructing students in manual and observational skills germane to the content of the lesson

- Developing knowledge of the scientific method

- Providing an opportunity to apply the scientific method to solving problems

- Creating a mentorship setting that might nurture professional attitudes

Brown and Atkins emphasize that students must view laboratory tasks as meaningful and pertinent.

I recall an excellent laboratory experience, a semester project in architecture that took students through a series of activities that included short lectures, studio activities, and a field project, exemplifying the true meaning of laboratory teaching and practical implementation. The instructor challenged the students to use what they had learned from his lectures by observing the downtown area of the city, where several buildings were empty and owners of other stores were considering leaving because of the popularity of the large shopping malls. The students sketched new storefronts that would-be shoppers might find more appealing. Next, the students actually created a small newspaper about downtown shopping, with their sketches of the storefronts, and distributed copies to the merchants and friends. Soon some of the merchants invested in new storefronts. The renewed downtown area began to draw residents back for dining and shopping. I can't think of a better application of laboratory teaching — relevant, meaningful, practical.

When using the laboratory method, the instructor must develop good communication and organization skills. Students must understand the goals and purposes of the lab experiences or chances will be reduced.

Research assistants and teaching assistants should feel at home in laboratory settings. It's useful for the instructor to spend time with the assistants in preparing the lab experiences. The instructor should discuss difficulties the assistants might encounter, help them prepare questions, and provide ideas for helping slower students. In preparing the assistants, the instructor also indirectly communicates the importance of laboratory experiences for the students. These interactions between instructor and graduate assistant represent a type of mentoring — preparing future professors for tomorrow's students.

Term Papers, Oral Reports, and Media

Brent and Felder (1992) advocate writing assignments that will promote deeper learning. They urge that instructors assign activities that move away from surface processing and simple memorization of information for examinations. They suggest that well-designed writing assignments can accomplish the following (p. 43):

- Encourage students to "explore their initial attitudes toward the subject to be studied"

- Stimulate students to "activate their prior knowledge about the subject"

- Lead students to "perceive the relevance of the subject to their lives and interests"

- Help students to "clarify, organize, and summarize course material"

- Stimulate students to "establish mental connections between newly learned and previously known material"

- Improve students' "critical thinking skills"

- Motivate students to "develop and strengthen their creativity"

Kamali (1991) presents six sequential steps that lead students to the completion of a term paper:

1. Getting started

2. Preliminary sketching

3. Critical thinking

4. Information-gathering

5. Analysis of the findings and concluding the study

6. Completing the semifinal draft

Barratt (1988) pleads for instructors to give more attention to formal writing and speaking and to how they relate directly to the students' personal environment. Writing papers and giving oral reports provide golden opportunities to build on the following points that Barratt believes everyone should learn (pp. 70-71):

- That language is legitimate
- That other people's language is legitimate
- That formal writing and formal speaking call for conventions different from those involved in informal uses
- That formal features of English are arbitrary
- That languages change
- That lack of knowledge and lack of formal language conventions are not the same
- That grammar can be developed at any time in any setting
- That language can be interesting

Term papers

Many instructors assign term papers. In fact, they're so much a part of higher education that they need little comment here.

But perhaps they're so important for some wrong reasons: some instructors feel that they're simply the "right way" to arrive at a grade for the students, while some students believe that instructors like term papers because they're easier to assign. So it may be worthwhile to recall several basic advantages of this traditional activity:

- Students increase their knowledge of a topic.
- Students learn how to use library and human resources.
- Students benefit from applying higher-level cognitive processes.
- Students learn how to organize their thoughts for others.

From term papers to oral reports

You can promote additional benefits by requiring oral reports about the term papers. A five-minute oral report on the salient points of a paper provides an opportunity for the student to practice the art of summarization and speaking skills. The student can also learn to direct discussions, if you add a question-and-answer session at the end of the report.

I observed an excellent use of this strategy in a construction management course that emphasized legal aspects from a lawyer's point of view. Each student was assigned a topic to pursue in depth during the semester and to apply what he or she learned to a fictitious company created by the instructor.

Near the end of the term, the instructor invited some colleagues to attend the class and role-play the president, vice president, comptroller, and board members for the fictitious company. Each student made a five-minute oral presentation about some legal aspect covered in the course, but within the context of the fictitious company.

For example, one student was very interested in the legal aspects of union and non-union contracts. In his presentation he recommended that the instructor's colleagues contract with unionized labor for a construction project. The instructor's colleagues then simulated their roles and asked the student penetrating questions, such as "What would happen if we hired a non-union group just to install the electricity and plumbing in the new building?" The student had to provide reasons to support his original recommendation, and he could reference studies that involved real legal battles that had taken place in similar situations. It was an excellent experience for the students.

Term papers represent still another way that instructors can take advantage of differences among students. A student may wish to pursue a topic in more depth, and the term paper's flexibility provides an opportunity for an instructor to capitalize on that high intrinsic motivation.

Media and materials

We have a vast array of media and materials to support our instructional efforts. I shall discuss those types that I believe a beginning instructor is most likely to encounter: multi-media, audio-tutorial, blackboard, and microcomputers.

Multi-Media Techniques. Sometimes the objectives for a lesson can best be reached by using videotaped programs, films, color slides, transparencies, radio programs, or telephone conversations. Of course, the objectives should always determine the choice of media, not the reverse.

- An oceanography instructor took a high-powered microscope and video camera to the Gulf of Mexico one summer so she could videotape organisms in their environment. She now plays those tapes in her oceanography course whenever her students are studying Gulf of Mexico organisms.

- An instructor in philosophy uses movies such as *Dead Poets Society* and *The Grapes of Wrath* as motivational introductions to selected topics in his values course.

- An instructor in soil and crop sciences uses 2"x2" color slides made from photographs of various grains so he can project pictures of the grains so all his students can view them simultaneously.

- A speech instructor likes to use tapes of old radio programs to highlight communication skills that enable listeners to conjure up their own images of scenes portrayed during broadcasts.

- A building and construction instructor enjoys arranging for a telephone conversation with an adjunct professor at a university in another state.

Color transparencies have become popular with many instructors. You could make a transparency of a chart, map, graph, photograph, etc. from a source other than the basic textbook and project it on a large screen during a lecture.

The whole arena of multi-media is vast, a broad topic that this book can't begin to cover. However, I would encourage you to either purchase a multi-media instructional textbook or go to the library and check out such a book to read and study.

If you are interested in multimedia, two excellent sources are *Multimedia for Learning: Development, Application, Evaluation* (Gayeski, 1993) and *Interactive Multimedia Instruction* (Schwier and Misanchuk, 1993). Both books provide information about the educational impact of Multimedia Development, HyperCard, CD Interactive, Digital Video Interactive (DVI), and Virtual Reality. Another book that covers the use of media in teaching is *Audio-visual Fundamentals: Basic Equipment Operation and Simple Materials Production* (Bullard and Mether, 1984).

Audio-Tutorial Programs. Postlethwait, Novak, and Murray (1969) developed one of the more successful programs that recognize and accommodate differences in students' rates of learning. It combined a variety of approaches that enabled biology students to use multiple senses to better learn course material. This is what Postlethwait does:

- He provides a weekly motivational lecture or invites a guest speaker to start that week's unit of study.

- He provides a handbook to accompany the program.

- He provides audio tapes, slides, and other media to accompany the lessons in his handbook.

- He arranges for space and resources for students to conduct experiments on an individual basis, if the lesson calls for experimentation.

- He requires students to progress through a weekly lesson at each student's own speed within an open laboratory setting where materials and tutors are available.

The Blackboard as Media. One of the best resources we have in our classrooms is the blackboard. Most classrooms have blackboards (sometimes greenboards or whiteboards) with chalk or colored markers and erasers. Using the board may seem simple — but sometimes we're not as thoughtful as we should be with this basic tool.

Organization is an important aspect in effective use of the board. There should be a logical flow of information as we write items on the board. Answer the following questions before you write on the board:

- What do I want my students to know at the end of the lesson?

- What should I select to put on the board?

- How should I organize my statements so they have some logic and reason for being highlighted on the board?

- When should I put the materials on the board? When should I erase them?

A few more guidelines when using the board:

- **Don't stand in front of your writing when lecturing.** Step aside so the students can see what you are referencing when discussing items on the board.

- **Don't be too quick to erase what you've written on the board.** Remember: it takes students more time to logically organize and process the information on the board than it takes us to put it there. Erase only the oldest information, after giving your students ample time to copy it.

- **Don't pack the board with too much information.** The key is to include only important information. And determine in advance the "board life" of your material: some items you may need for only a few minutes, while others should remain on the board for the entire class session.

- **Be the student.** Sit in the seat farthest from the board. Make sure you write or print large enough for students to see from the back of the room. Are there any intervening obstacles, such as an overhead projector, lectern, boxes on tables, etc. that might obstruct their view of the board?

- **Write legibly.** If your writing is terrible, print. The students won't benefit from your preparation if they can't decipher your writing. Be careful to write out the whole word instead of using shortened forms to save time. Students often write only the shortened forms — which they may no longer understand when they review their notes.

- **Plan for your space.** Try to visualize the space you'll need on the board, or actually sketch on paper the items you want to put on the board, so you have some idea about how much space they will take. Remember: students are generally taking notes on vertical, 8½"x11" sheets of paper, while you are using a horizontal board of quite different dimensions.

Some instructors enter the classroom ahead of schedule and lightly outline any sketches they are going to make during a lesson. Then when they arrive at the point in the lecture when they need the sketch, they can draw heavily over the light outline or perhaps use colored chalk to highlight the sketch.

- **Avoid unnecessary competition.** Sometimes what you put on the board may distract students from what you're saying five minutes later.

Microcomputers. What an impact the microcomputer has had on education, from elementary through graduate school and beyond! Instructors in the '90s should make the most of our computer opportunities. Computers can:

- Help improve study skills

- Tutor students at their own pace through well-designed problem-solving activities

- Simulate experiences from the world of work

- Present material through text, graphics, and sound — simultaneously

- Allow students to network with other students and scholars around the globe

Instructors at Texas A&M University have used incentive grants from the university's Center for Teaching Excellence to help them develop some very innovative microcomputer programs. They report that the time involved in developing microcomputer programs is worth the effort.

What are the possibilities in the college setting? Here are some:

- A rule-based, computer-aided design package could help students design structures in architecture or engineering.

- A series of interactive question-and-answer sessions could quiz students in cellular physiology and neurophysiology.

- A data base for general pathology could allow medical students to select a body part on the screen and progressively focus in on that part of the body, just as they would increase the power of a microscope.

- In chemistry labs, self-instructional programs can provide students with immediate feedback and reinforcement.

- Computerized case studies in clinical chemistry can enrich and supplement the curriculum.

- In foreign languages, testing programs, simulations, and word games can greatly enhance classroom experiences — and electronic mail can connect students with native speakers of the languages they are studying.

- Computer applications can be used in teaching, writing, and literature.

- Nursing students can use software to help develop their ability to calculate medication dosages.

- Business students can use software to implement practical experience in solving simple problems.

- Programs can present steps in the diagnostic reasoning process, recognition of relevant and irrelevant cues, and linking cues to clinical situations for students.

- In physics classes programs can help students develop the scientific method approach in solving problems.

- Instructors in biology can use computers to teach students how to collect, retrieve, analyze information, and draw conclusions.

Kettinger (1991) describes the computer classroom as having tremendous potential in improving learning. He then presents reasons why the potential hasn't been realized:

1. Failure to provide incentives and rewards for engaging in innovative efforts

2. Lack of quality instructional software

3. Unresponsive administrators

4. The short supply of quality research to support implementation of computer classrooms

Farrow (1993) describes a program at the University of South Australia in which students were each assigned a different neurological condition to pursue through reading research studies and the literature, to prepare a tutorial for presentation at the end of the course. While reviewing literature and research, the students were instructed in the techniques required to develop a HyperCard program. She reports that the HyperCard project provided a great learning experience and gave the students a different set of insights into neurological conditions.

Rae (1993) made an interesting adaptation using the Keller Plan. While following the basic structure of the original Keller Plan (see Chapter 7), he complements it with video tapes, interactive videodiscs, and computerized tutorials.

Graesser and Person (1994, p. 129) point out:

> Computer software has recently been designed to permit extensive question asking by the learner ... through a 'Point and Query' (P&Q) system [that] radically facilitates the speed and quality of questioning. ... The student learns entirely by asking questions and reading answers. To ask a question, the student first points to a word or picture element on the computer screen and then to a question that is relevant to the element (from a menu of relevant questions). ... The P&Q software is embedded in a hypertext system, so answers are preformulated and quickly accessed; the student can ask a question with two points of a finger (or two clicks of a mouse).

Instructional technology is constant changing. The teaching journals in your discipline should provide you with current information on what is available. In addition, the *Chronicle of Higher Education* reviews instructional software regularly. If you want to elicit recommendations from colleagues in your discipline around the world, you might try posting a query to Internet discussion lists.

Evaluating Your Students

Evaluation is a common task confronting instructors, but it shouldn't be taken lightly. The most common means — tests — serve three major purposes:

- They provide a record of data so the instructor can assign grades to the students.

- They provide a learning experience for the students: the results enable them to correct their misunderstandings or to seek help from the instructor.

- They motivate students. Anytime I announced that there would be a test on Friday covering the first three chapters of the basic text, students read and reviewed those chapters — some for the first time.

Prerequisite testing

A number of instructors administer prerequisite assessment tests during the first week of classes. This form of testing serves an important purpose: to determine if the students enrolled in the course have the prerequisite knowledge to succeed. The steps involved are:

1. Develop a set of objectives for the course, listing what you want the students to be able to do when they complete the course.

2. Determine what prerequisite skills and knowledge will be required for the students to complete the course successfully.

3. Develop a diagnostic test to measure those prerequisite skills and knowledge.

4. Tell the students why you are administering the prerequisite test and inform them that it doesn't count for a grade.

For example, a math course may require knowledge about polynomial arithmetic before the student can master a specific course objective.

Therefore, the prerequisite test needs to include diagnostic items on exponents, combining similar terms, the distributive property, binomials, simplifying polynomials, and division of polynomials. If any students can't handle those items, the instructor should advise them to enroll in a prerequisite course, although some students may be able to continue if they have difficulty only with division of polynomials, for example.

Testing during the second week

Another approach that you might consider is to develop a battery of test items over course content, based on your set of objectives. Then, the second week of the course, you could administer the battery of items, informing the students that the test doesn't count for a grade, although students who reach your predetermined success level could receive credit. This type of test serves the following purposes:

1. If students have the prerequisite knowledge and skills and have already reached your predetermined success level for the course, you could arrange for independent enrichment activities, rather than bore them with information that they have mastered already, or you could advise them to drop your course and take a more advanced course.

2. If the course is organized as a self-instructional program around weekly units of study, analysis of the data could help you place the better students in the appropriate self-instructional modules. For example, if you have 16 modules organized in a linear manner, you may decide that one student could skip the first seven modules and begin with the eighth, while another student may begin with the third module, and so forth.

3. If your course is organized as lectures and your analysis reveals that most of the students are strong in some content areas but weak in others, you may emphasize the content where the data indicate weaknesses and bypass or touch lightly on content that students already appear to know.

Testing during the course

You may want to administer quizzes throughout the entire semester to determine if the students are progressing toward completion of the objectives and to identify any problems in the course. Quizzes may reveal a need to backtrack and review material with additional examples and illustrations. Through periodic quizzes, you can identify the students who would benefit from corrective measures before those students fall too far behind.

First Steps to Excellence in College Teaching

I believe that quizzes and grades provide external motivation for some students. Moreover, they can be powerful learning experiences — if the test situation provides opportunities for students to recall information, reorganize thoughts, and use higher cognitive processes. Therefore, frequent testing can help students reinforce what they have learned: if the tests are good, preparing for them requires the students to review what they've studied.

Testing at the end of the course

If the students pass the final exam, they should feel comfortable moving into the next module or course of study because they know they have the prerequisite knowledge and skills to succeed.

However, analysis of final examination data may lead you to revise your course, if large numbers of students are not reaching acceptable levels of success. If they are typical students, and no extenuating reasons can be detected for their failure to achieve, then you should review your materials, procedures, learning activities, instructional strategies, and attitude to see if changes may be necessary.

Norm-referenced testing

Norm-referenced testing involves a system for evaluating and grading students in relation to their peers. A student's effort from one test to another is not considered in this type of testing, because the test is intended to discriminate among students. Grades are usually assigned on the basis of the normal curve, which assumes that the achievement of the students is distributed normally.

There are some limitations to norm-referenced testing:

1. Two sections of the same course may be divided in such a way that more of the brighter, more knowledgeable students are enrolled in one section. Use of norms will penalize some intelligent, knowledgeable students in the first section because there are more comparable students in that section. Less knowledgeable, less intelligent students in the second section will receive higher scores than students with the same knowledge and intelligence in the first section.

2. Scores alone do not communicate the level of knowledge and skills attained by the students in the course. Students become the reference point, not their knowledge of content or their level of performance skills. If 70 is the highest score on the exam, for example, the normal curve converts the score to an A — unless the

instructor sets minimums, such as "no A's for scores under 90 and no B's for scores under 80."

Criterion-referenced testing

To avoid the above limitations of norm-referenced testing, some instructors use criterion-referenced testing. Criterion-referenced testing involves a predetermined set of performance statements that students pursue without relation to their peers. The achievement statement must be quite precise, since the instructor does not assign certain percentages of A's, B's, C's, D's and F's. All students could receive an A on a test if they reach the predetermined set of performance statements.

A criterion-referenced statement might be, for example, "The student will identify all three branches of government" or "The student will run a 100-meter dash in less than 12 seconds." The student who responds correctly or who beats the time receives 100% or A on that part of the test. This process continues throughout the entire test, with credit given for reaching each predetermined acceptable performance level.

Criterion-referenced testing also has limitations:

1. As mentioned above, all the students could receive A's on the test or for the course. This drives some registrars, administrators, and faculty crazy because they are used to a spread in grades, a discrimination among students in the course. They may not understand or accept criterion-based approaches to evaluation, although business has used such assessment for decades — either a salesperson sells $300,000 in computers during the year or he or she gets fired; either the widget meets a predetermined specification or it doesn't pass quality control; either the hamburgers are sold within X minutes after cooking or they're discarded.

2. Since criterion-referenced testing doesn't require discriminating among students, a prospective employer or a graduate school has no way of knowing how a particular student compares with his or her counterparts.

3. Some students who could finish a course by getting D's on norm-referenced tests may not complete a criterion-referenced course because they fail to meet a predetermined mastery level on the tests. Some instructors give such students a grade of "Incomplete"; they must then retake the course until they reach the acceptable level of performance — or find an instructor who uses norm-referenced testing.

Criterion-referenced tests appear to go well with mastery-learning programs, since they have absolute standards for acceptable performance.

Types of tests

There are a number of different types of tests and evaluation procedures. In this section I will discuss essay tests, completion tests, matching tests, true/false tests, and multiple-choice tests.

Essay Tests. Essay tests are well-suited for assessing the ability to use higher cognitive processes. They provide students with an opportunity to interpret information and make generalizations in given situations.

When using essay tests, you should consider several factors. You need to determine and announce in advance the criteria you will use in grading. The criteria may include:

- Content
- Coherence
- Relevance (dealing only with the topic)
- Good writing
- Correct spelling
- Legibility

You should discuss the criteria with your students before they prepare for the test, so they understand the grading procedures and have a better idea of how to prepare for the test.

When the essay test consists of more than one question, you should require your students to respond to all of the items. This provides you with a common reference point. If you allow students to "select two of the three questions," for example, you may make inaccurate assumptions. For example, Sally may have been prepared for all three questions, but Jean may not know anything about question number two. Yet, because they have the right to select two of the three questions, you might wrongly conclude that Sally and Jean are equally competent.

Essay tests may be easier to develop than good objective types of tests, but essay tests are more difficult and time-consuming to grade. You must also consider reliability in grading. Some classic studies have revealed that professors from the same discipline assigned grades ranging from A to F on identical essays; if you place a typed list of criteria alongside each student's paper during the grading, this point of reference helps reduce time and variations.

Also, before grading essays, fold each student's name under, to hide it while you're reading the paper: this helps prevent "halo" influences. For example, if you see Shana's name on the paper, you might give it a higher score than it deserves simply because Shana is a very bright student who agrees with you during class. Or a paper with Mike's name might get a better grade simply because Mike always smiles in class.

No, this technique isn't foolproof; with time you might begin to recognize the handwriting of students. However, it's worth considering.

If you really want to minimize "halo" influences, use pseudonyms:

1. On the first day, ask each student to choose a pseudonym, then to write or type the pseudonym and his or her real name on an index card.

2. Collect the cards and place them in an envelope, seal it, then set it aside until the end of the course.

3. Have each student turn in another index card with just his or her pseudonym. Use these cards to list the pseudonyms in your grade book.

4. Have the students use their pseudonyms on all tests and written assignments.

5. Score the tests or assignments and record the grades in your grade book. At the close of the next class session, set the papers out on your table or desk, then depart so that the students can maintain their pseudonymity as they retrieve them.

6. At the close of the course, when you've determined all the final grades, open the sealed envelope and match the grades with the real names.

Of course, it may not be possible for you to use pseudonyms in your course because you want to meet each student personally, because you want each student to feel free to confer with you about any test or assignment, or because you include oral exercises or class participation in their grades.

The following are examples of essay questions:

- List and discuss what you consider to be three major reasons for the North defeating the South during the Civil War. Support your answers by referencing primary and secondary sources.
- Discuss three reasons for supporting wildlife conservation. Support your reasons.

- Compare and contrast three political ideologies in the U.S.

- Explain why it is important for building construction students to know and understand the legal aspects involved in a contract to build a government building.

When grading essay exams, most authorities on testing recommend reading all of the essays for the first question before proceeding to the essays for the second question. They also recommend reading the essays for each question twice.

After the first reading of the essays for the first question (using your reference list of criteria), sort the papers into five stacks, putting the best essays in the first stack and the poorest essays in the fifth stack. Put the others in the middle three stacks, setting those that are closer to the best in the second stack and those that are closer to the poorest in the fourth stack. Now you will have five common reference points.

Then read all essays a second time and make any suitable adjustments of the papers: on a second reading, an essay may appear better or worse than you first judged it and you may decide to move it to another stack. Eventually, you assign grades to the essays. You could assign A's to stack one, B's to stack two, C's to stack three, D's to stack four, and F's to stack five. If you believe that all of the papers in stacks four and five deserve the higher grade, give them all D's. This is where subjective grading takes place, as you assign the grades you consider appropriate for the first essay, in relation to others in the same stack.

Next, read all essays for the second question, following the same procedure, and so on for all the questions. Finally, you will have to assign an overall grade for each student's total number of essays.

Completion Tests. Sentence-completion tests, sometimes called short-answer tests, require students to use a word or phrase to complete a statement. Be very careful when constructing sentence-completion tests. When the students read the sentence, they should have no difficulty understanding what response you are seeking. To help eliminate ambiguity, have a few colleagues and/or former students read an item, then ask them for their reactions: "Did you have difficulty understanding any part of the sentence? Did you know the answer I was seeking? What was it?"

Another recommendation is to place the fill-in space in a location other than as the first or last words of the statement. The closer to the middle, the better — but not at the risk of coherence. This procedure enables the student to take full advantage of contextual cues.

Completion tests are particularly valuable if you want the students to move from recall of exact words to the next higher level of the cognitive domain, comprehension. The test can require students to use their own words to show what they've learned.

You can establish points for each correct response. Difficult items geared to very important objectives might be worth five points each, while items for less important objectives may be worth one point each. The point value for each item should be identified on the test; the directions might indicate that the first 15 items have a value of five points each, while the remaining 25 items have a value of one point each, for a total of 100 points.

The following are examples of completion items:

1. President John F. Kennedy approved the Bay of Pigs invasion, during which _____ made up the main forces landing on the beaches of Cuba.

2. During Lyndon B. Johnson's first campaign for the U.S. Senate, _____ served as his advisor, close associate, and campaign manager.

Be sure to provide enough space for the completion and to make all of the spaces of equal length. Also, word the item so as to exclude all but the correct completion. Consider item 1 above: since students could put "soldiers" or "Americans" or even just "people" in the blank, the item would not adequately test what the students have learned.

Matching Items Tests. A matching items test consists of two related lists of words, symbols, pictures, or statements. Matching tests are very useful when you've emphasized dates, events, locations, treaties, and persons: you can quickly and effectively measure the ability of the students to recall and associate such items.

Items in the first (left) column are known as the *premises*. Items in the second (right) column are known as the *responses*.

A few recommendations:

- Keep the items in each list homogeneous — all names, all dates, all numbers, all places, and so forth.

- Make sure there's only one correct response for each item to be matched.

- Put all options in both columns on the same page, so students don't need to flip pages back and forth.

- If names make up a list, put them in alphabetical order, last name first (e.g., Roosevelt, Franklin D.), so students can locate premises and responses.

- If you list dates or numbers, place them in either descending or ascending order: don't jumble them.

- Put several extra items in the response column, to prevent matching by process of elimination.

On the following two pages are examples of matching tests.

True/False Tests. True/false tests are advantageous when objectives for the course involve knowledge and comprehension of a very large number of facts. Another advantage is the ease in scoring. In fact, a secretary or assistant could grade a true/false test for you.

A major disadvantage is that students have a 50-50 chance of guessing the correct responses. Another limitation in developing a good true/false exam is the difficulty in avoiding ambiguity. Avoid using the following words: *never, always, usually, sometimes, all, only, generally, frequently.*

Other recommendations for true/false tests:

- Make the length of both true and false statements similar.

- Identify an equal number of "true" items and "false" items.

- Use your own words in the test items, not the same as in the textbook.

- Refrain from using double negatives or tricky wording.

- Underline negatives used in the items.

- Randomize the order of the items, so a pattern doesn't emerge (e.g., 10 true, then 10 false, then 10 true).

The following is an example of a true/false item:

> **Directions.** Circle T if the statement is more true than false; circle F if the statement is more false than true.
>
> 1. **T F** Dwight D. Eisenhower served as president of the United States from 1953 into 1961.

Multiple-Choice Tests. Multiple-choice tests are flexible and can be used to test students over a large body of information. Most are either four-option or five-option, although the specific content often dictates the potential number of choices you can use.

The following is an example of a multiple-choice test item:

Sample Test

1. Match each president's name in the first column with the dates of office in the second column by writing the number of the matching item on the line to the left of each president's name:

_____ Adams, John   1. 1789-1797

_____ Buchanan, James   2. 1797-1801

_____ Fillmore, Millard   3. 1807-1809

_____ Jackson, Andrew   4. 1809-1817

_____ Madison, James   5. 1817-1825

_____ Monroe, James   6. 1825-1829

_____ Pierce, Franklin   7. 1829-1837

_____ Polk, James K.   8. 1837-1841

_____ Tyler, John   9. 1841-1845

_____ Van Buren, Martin   10. 1845-1849

                                       11. 1849-1850

                                       12. 1850-1853

                                       13. 1853-1857

                                       14. 1857-1861

                                       15. 1861-1865

Sample Test

2. Match the descriptions of the treaties, agreements, and organizations in the left column with the acronyms (all caps) in the right column by writing the number of the matching item on the line to the left of each description:

_____ Thailand, Malaysia, Singapore, Indonesia, and the Philippines formed this non-military alliance in 1967.

_____ This defense shield on the northern tier of the Middle East was formed in 1955 to protect against a Soviet penetration.

_____ Formed in 1959 by Austria, Iceland, Norway, Portugal, Sweden, Switzerland, and Finland, this organization was established to generate economic growth and equitable competition .

_____ In 1949, this powerful organization was formed as a regional defense for the North Atlantic area.

_____ Most of the countries in North, Central, and South America created this organization in 1948.

1. EFTA

2. SOA

3. CENTO

4. AEASN

5. OTNA

6. TFAE

7. OAS

8. CNOTE

9. ASEAN

10. NATO

1. The first president of the United States was:
   a. Thomas Jefferson
   b. John Quincy Adams
   c. George Washington
   d. None of the above

You should keep a record of your test items from semester to semester. Place each multiple-choice test item on an index card. On the reverse side of the card, place certain data you may wish for reference purposes, e.g., the correct response, the date you used the item on a test, the number of students who took the test, and the number who answered the item correctly.

Let's consider our example again. The main section (the *stem*) spells out the task. After reading the stem, the student should know what to do before reading the choices (the *options*). Only one option should be the correct response. The other options (*distracters*) should be homogeneous, i.e., they should have promise as possible answers. For example, don't ask the students to identify the 16th president of the United States, and then list as the distracters such names as Marilyn Monroe, Henry Ford, and Ben Franklin. You should list as choices four presidents who served between 1830 and 1864.

The stem should:

- Be brief, yet complete

- Reflect only one main idea

- Form a grammatical unit with each of the options

- Not give away the correct answer, e.g., it shouldn't call for an answer in the plural while all of the options but one are singular

Test construction

Use your course objectives as the foundation in developing your tests. Once you've written your objectives, decide how much to stress each objective during the course. Give a weight to the value of each objective. For example, if you have four objectives, you might feel that the first objective is worth twice as much as any other of the remaining three objectives; give it 40% of the test emphasis, with a 20% emphasis for each of the remaining three objectives.

Validity, reliability, and practicality are additional factors to consider when constructing your tests.

Validity. This factor refers to the degree to which the test measures what it is purported to measure. The following are a few ways to check the validity of evaluation instruments:

- Cross-reference the items with textbooks, journals, and research reports to see if the items stress basic, current material.

- Discuss the items with colleagues; ask them if they think the items are important in evaluating students.

- If feasible, ask professionals in the discipline — former students and prospective employers — if mastery of the items is important for success in the field.

Reliability. This factor refers to the consistency and accuracy of student responses to test items each time the test is administered. In other words, the student's response to a test item should be basically the same if he or she completed the test today and again tomorrow without intervening variables such as learning, forgetting, illness, or emotional upset.

Reliability can be checked by using alternate forms of the same instrument, particularly if you teach multiple sections of the same course. You want consistency — the same results or basic agreement among the different sections. Students in section one could complete form A of the test, while students in section two could complete form B. On the second administration, section one would complete form B, while section two would complete form A. Simple correlation coefficient statistics can be used to demonstrate similarity in the results from two different administrations of the same test to the same students (called test-retest method).

Practicality. This factor refers to compiling, administering, scoring, time, and cost factors. Can the evaluation instrument be developed, administered, and scored within the limitations of time and resource constraints?

Check practicality by answering the following questions:

- Which type of test will efficiently measure student progress toward the objectives in a valid, reliable way?

- Do I have the time and resources to develop and to grade this particular type of test?

- Do the students have time to complete the test?

Test item analysis

Test items should be analyzed to determine if they are positive or negative discriminators. If more students with high overall test scores marked an item incorrectly than those with low overall test scores, the item had *negative* discrimination — it's open to question. If more students with high overall test scores marked an item correctly than those with low overall test scores, the item had *positive* discrimination. Build a file of positive discriminating items, for use in future tests. Either revise or discard negative discriminating items.

The following is a simple method for determining positive or negative discrimination and index difficulty — "easiness of the item" — i.e., how difficult is the item for the average student in your course?

Identify the 10 papers with the highest overall test scores and the 10 papers with the lowest overall test scores. Then, prepare an item analysis sheet as follows:

Item #	H	L	H+L	H-L	Comment
1					
2					
3					
4					
*					
*					
50					

The column headings of the item analysis sheet are interpreted as follows:

H =   number of 10 highest-scoring students answering the test item correctly

L =   number of 10 lowest-scoring students answering the test item correctly

H+L = number from both high and low groups answering the test item correctly

H-L = number of high-scoring students minus the number of low-scoring students answering the test item correctly

If the figure in the H-L column is minus for an item, that indicates a negative discrimination: the item needs revision. If the figure in the H-L column is plus, that indicates positive discrimination.

Let's assume that on test item #1 all 10 of the highest-scoring students selected the correct response, while six of the lowest-scoring students did. Our item analysis would appear as follows:

Item #	H	L	H+L	H-L	Comment
1	10	6	16	+4	positive

Some instructors believe that an index difficulty of between 7 and 17 is desirable for the H+L column and an index of +3 or above for the H-L column. Personally, I've used test items with a zero index for the H-L column and an index difficulty between 18 and 20 for the H+L column. If such an item reinforces learning and rewards students, I am in favor of keeping it for future tests.

You should also check test reliability. A quick and easy way is to use a scattergram (examples appear in Figures 9.1, 9.2, and 9.3), based on split halves of an entire test:

1. Divide the test into two parts, with even-numbered items (2, 4, 6, 8 ... 100) representing one half of the test and odd-numbered items (1, 3, 5, 7 ... 99) representing the other half of the test. This is preferable to using items 1 through 50 as part one and items 51 through 100 as part two, since not all students may complete the final items, or some may become fatigued toward the end of the exam.

2. Design a scattergram like the one displayed in Figure 9.1.

   Look at student #1's score for the first test half (the odd-numbered items, 1-99) and his score for the second test half (the even-numbered items, 2-100). Place a dot where his two scores intersect on the scattergram; if he had 50 correct on the first half and 48 correct on the second half, the dot would be to the right of 48 on the axis for part two and directly vertical of a score of 50 for the first half. (See dot in Figure 9.1.)

   The dot for student #1 would be slightly to the right of the diagonal line. The greater the number of dots following close to the diagonal line, the greater the inference for a reliable test.

Look at the scattergram in Figure 9.2. There appears to be a high positive correlation, which probably means the test has high reliability.

Look at the third scattergram (Figure 9.3). There is a negative correlation, which suggests that something is wrong with the reliability of the test.

I have found it satisfactory for my own use to merely scan the scattergram, but other instructors may prefer the more detailed procedures of the Kuder-Richardson Formula 20, Cronbach's Coefficient Alpha, and the Pearson-Moment Coefficient of Correlation for computing the reliability of a test. These are explained in most introductory statistics books, such as Borg and Gall, *Educational Research*, 1989.

Test administration

Another important consideration is the setting in which you evaluate your students. Environmental conditions influence performance: temperature and ventilation, seating arrangements, lighting, noise level, test materials, directions, and follow-up activities are all important.

Be sure the room is well-ventilated and at a comfortable temperature. You may need to check the room earlier in the day in order to have appropriate personnel adjust the thermostat setting. Personnel can also replace burned out or flickering lights; bad fluorescent tubes drive some people crazy!

If possible, arrange the seating in such a way that the students and you feel comfortable. Students should not be crowded and should not be able to see each other's tests.

Figure 9.1

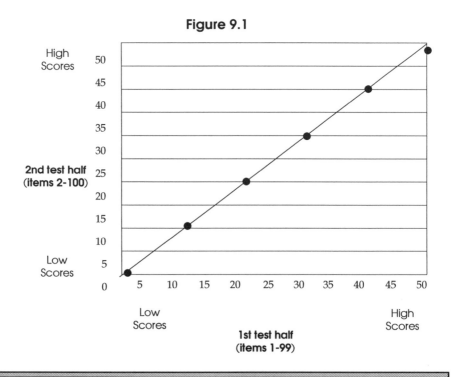

You can reduce the possibility of cheating on tests by following these suggestions:

- Revise tests periodically.
- Number all test booklets so you'll know if any are missing at the end of the test period.
- Spread out the chairs.
- Monitor the testing room.
- Use different forms of the same test with different sections of the course.
- Rearrange the order of test items for odd- and even-numbered test booklets.

There are a few other recommendations to consider. Since the type of test expected by the students influences their preparation, it seems appropriate to tell the students in advance about the type of test. Why expect the students to "outguess" the instructor? After all, we're not evaluating extrasensory perception!

Research findings support the idea of providing space between test items so anxious students have a chance to make comments. The procedure

Figure 9.2

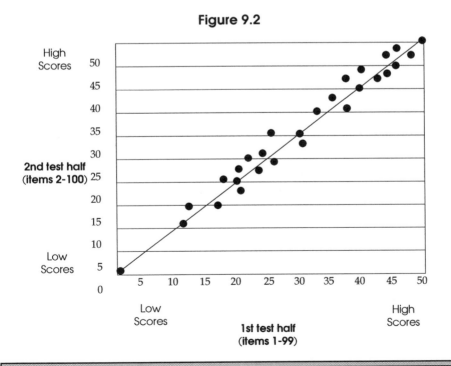

Figure 9.3

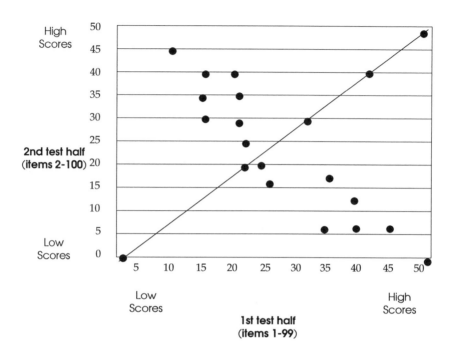

Figure 9.3

reduces student anxiety. A student can write, "This item stinks!" and then go on to obtain overall higher scores than do anxious students who have no opportunities to release their negative feelings.

Test directions should be clear. You should review the procedures at the beginning of the class to avoid confusion, correct typographical errors, check to see that each student has all pages or materials required, answer questions, and discuss scoring procedures. Ask the students to write their names on all pages, in case the pages become separated. Be sensitive, straightforward, and brief. Guide, but don't hold their hands or waste their time.

Grading

Some of the most effective learning takes place after the test. Grade the test as soon as possible, and discuss the results with students during the first class meeting following the grading. Discussion provides feedback and reinforces learning. It also helps you discover weaknesses in specific test items or in the test in general. Be sure to keep individual test results confidential; you don't want to embarrass any students who did poorly or who did well, by pointing them out in class. Their papers provide a suitable place for any comments, questions, and compliments.

Grades are summative symbols that instructors use to tell how students have performed. Judgments may be intuitive and subjective (e.g., scores assigned to essay responses) or mechanical and objective (e.g., sum of all scores from a series of multiple-choice tests, rank-ordered, with the top 20% of the scores receiving an A).

Even with objective tests, however, personal biases intrude upon your "objective" judgments. Did the multiple-choice tests represent the best basis for ranking the students? Were all the items suitable as evidence that students had achieved the course objectives? Were the responses that you accepted as correct the only appropriate responses for the test items? Was it appropriate for only 20% of the students to receive an A?

The grading system must be simple, yet it must communicate academic achievement effectively to students, parents, administrators, employers, counselors, and personnel in other institutions, including graduate schools.

Some institutions attempt to ensure grading uniformity by having their instructors reach a consensus on the meaning of grades in relation to a standard group of students. For example, some may agree that an A means that the student was in the top 15% of the students in the course, B means that the student was in the next 25%, C means that the student was in the next 40%, and so forth.

One source suggests the following interesting way of communicating the meaning of grades:

A = all major and minor objectives achieved

A- = almost all major and minor objectives achieved

B+ = most major and minor objectives achieved

B = most major objectives achieved, some minor objectives not achieved

C+ = most major objectives achieved, several minor objectives not achieved

C = some major objectives and some minor objectives achieved, but not most of both

D = student is not prepared for advanced work

F = failed the course

How does an instructor or a department establish a grading system if one doesn't exist? What should be considered when establishing the system?

I would recommend beginning by determining the specific purposes to be served by a grading system. The more important purposes include the following:

- To guide the students
- To help the department determine if a student should continue in its program of study
- To indicate to other institutions what success a student might have, as a transfer or graduate student
- To provide a reference point for prospective employers

I'd encourage you to determine in advance the acceptable performance level for students in the course. I'd recommend that the performance level be directly related to your course objectives. At the undergraduate level, I would recommend that an acceptable performance level always be considered a C, with the following qualifiers:

- A range of performance levels above "acceptable" exists, so an ample number of students may achieve B's and A's.
- The standard curve has been rejected.
- Grades are accepted as relative, not absolute, since our reference points are not absolutely clear and dependable.

I'd also encourage you to administer a typical exam on a "use or throw away" basis during the first three weeks of the course. The exam should be real, for credit, but the students should have the right to throw out this first test.

Why? The first test provides early feedback to you and your students. The "use or throw away" option provides students an opportunity to recover from a devastating score. They might receive a poor grade on the first exam because they didn't perceive what the test would require, or didn't understand what you expected, or underestimated the level of preparation needed.

By obtaining early feedback from the first examination, the students can take corrective measures and receive a final grade that would better reflect their ability — which wouldn't happen if the low grade were retained.

However, in the final exam for the course I believe that you should include some new test items that reflect the objectives that you had in mind for the first test. The students who "threw away" their first test scores must still be held accountable for achieving your objectives for that part of the course.

Murray (1990) likes giving students a second chance to learn by giving the test in class, then handing the student a copy of the same test to take home to complete a second time. He is convinced that students learn more when they engage in immediate self-feedback following the in-class test.

If you are interested in more in-depth coverage of testing, you might review the following references:

Robert Ladd Thorndike and Elizabeth P. Hagen, *Measurement and Evaluation in Psychology and Education*, 1977.

Anne Anastasi, *Psychological Testing*, 1988.

Walter R. Borg and Meredith Damien Gall, *Educational Research*, 1989.

Portfolios

Portfolios, an alternative assessment technique that has been used in art and architecture for years, has recently found followers among instructors in such disciplines as medicine, law, business, and education, who consider them a more "authentic" evaluation process.

Instructors use the portfolios instead of tests. Students are required to place in their portfolios samples of their best work as they perceive it to represent achievement of course goals and objectives. These samples may take a variety of forms: e.g., a review of a book or film or television show, a written report on the results of an experiment, a description of a trip to a courthouse to view a court in session, a compilation of an observational study of wild turkeys in the fields, and so forth.

Students will need some guidance to determine what should go into their portfolios. It might be best to establish a specific set of categories of samples that would reflect the goals and objectives of the course.

Lynn Burlbaw, a professor at Texas A&M University, uses portfolios when teaching undergraduate and graduate students. He claims that portfolios help students evaluate their learning and progress in the courses.

In his undergraduate course, the students collect readings they did for the course, test questions they developed, and planning notes and activities written in a log. Near the end of the semester, students write a self-evaluation essay documenting what they have learned about learning and about themselves as learners, the content of the course, and ways they would change their semester activities if they had to do it again. Students refer to specific materials in their portfolios to document the points they make in their essays.

In a graduate course, his students collected articles related to course readings, wrote summaries and critiques of readings and articles, and at the end of the semester reflected upon what they had learned as a result of their reading. They also graded their semester performance and justified the grade through the materials in the portfolio. In another assignment, "Writing for Publication," students retained all drafts, versions, critiques, and submissions of an article written during the semester. By reading over the contents in this portfolio, students could see how their ideas had developed, changed, and matured during the course of the semester.

Stahle and Mitchell (1993) believe that an even more valuable outcome can be achieved if the instructor will have each student read the other students' portfolios.

Starr (1991) uses the microcomputer network to review students' papers. The students must submit their papers to Starr via the network, and he adds his suggestions to the student's paper by placing comments within brackets, e. g., [at this point you need to elaborate on why you are taking this position]. He then routes the paper back to the student's "network mailbox."

Starr believes that his approach has the following benefits (pp. 56-58):

- It prepares students for the real world, where microcomputers are widely used.

- It enables the instructor to suggest changes in great detail and exactly where he or she would wish to make the changes.

- It speeds up the feedback process and the grading process.

- It probably reduces errors.

Brown (1991) requires students to create and submit three questions each week. The weekly critique of the questions for structure and content revealed excellent progress and stimulated student participation in the classroom.

Cameron (1991) offers an interesting suggestion. She believes that instructors should label questions with the specific thinking skills required to answer the questions. That might also help students improve their metacognitive skills.

Test anxiety

Someone once remarked that the ideal instructor is someone who has survived years of text anxiety — with the only casualty being his or her memory of it. That comment seems more clever than correct: many instructors worry a great deal about the anxiety experienced by their students when faced with tests.

Some have devoted time and energy to studying test anxiety. O'Brien (1991) reviews several of those research studies, to conclude that instructional strategies are important in reducing test anxiety. Mealey and Host (1992) believe that test anxiety is caused by the lack of preparation, negative thoughts during testing, and an erroneous belief that poor test preparation strategies are adequate. They suggest that instructors should help students with learning strategies and metacognitive strategies. They recommend self-questioning, mapping, and text annotation as helpful to students. They also suggest that some students need a non-threatening classroom environment when learning and when taking examinations and that instructors can help reduce test anxiety:

- Don't interrupt students during testing.
- Conduct a review session prior to the test.
- Don't walk around the room looking over the shoulders of the students.
- Give the students positive reinforcement and don't lead them to believe the test will be overly difficult.

Conclusion

You have to evaluate your students, to provide them with at least three things — a learning experience, additional external motivation, and most likely grades. But you probably are free to choose means that are appropriate and not likely to cause unnecessary anxiety. We encourage you to exercise that freedom and to explore the possibilities!

A Teaching Creed

by Glenn Ross Johnson

I f you are a beginning instructor, I wish you well in your pursuit of excellence in teaching. I would like to leave you with the following Teaching Creed that I wrote and distributed to all faculty members, teaching assistants, and administrators at my institution when I opened the new instructional development center. Place it in a handy location so you can start your day with the Teaching Creed as a reminder of what you are striving to accomplish.

Although I recognize there are many different ways to teach, I believe our students are entitled to college teachers who strive to accomplish the following:

- Be well-versed in the knowledge of their subject matter.

- Be well-prepared for classes.

- Remain sincerely interested in what they teach.

- Use teaching methods which are in line with course objectives.

- Administer meaningful and well-constructed examinations.

- Remain fair and reasonable in evaluation students.

- Encourage intelligent, independent thought by students.

- Treat students with respect within and outside the classroom.

- Respond to questions to the best of their ability.

- Try to motivate students with a variety of examples and illustrations that show a practical application of content.

Appendix

SYLLABUS FOR EDCI 601: "COLLEGE TEACHING"

SPRING 1995
Dr. Glenn Ross Johnson
Mondays 12:40 p.m. - 3:30 p.m.
EDCT 371

Special Notes:

Phone: (409) 845-8053

Fax: 409/845-9663

Internet: E102GJ@TAMVM1.TAMU.EDU

Office: 1:00 p.m. - 2:00 p.m., Tuesdays/Thursdays; other times by appointment

Escort Service at night for women: Campus Police 845-2345. (Also, the Corps of Cadets provides such a service.)

The Americans with Disabilities Act (ADA) is a federal anti-discrimination statute that provides comprehensive civil rights protection for persons with disabilities. Among other things, this legislation requires that all students with disabilities be guaranteed a learning environment that provides for reasonable accommodation of their disabilities. If you believe you have a disability requiring an accommodation, please contact the Office of Support Services for Students with Disabilities in Room 126 of the Student Services Building. The phone number is 845-1637.

If you are willing, I would appreciate knowing if you have any physical, medical, mental, or learning disabilities. This information may assist me in accommodating for diversity among our students.

Class/Session	Date	Topics	Presenter/Faciltator
1	Jan. 23	Logistics	Johnson
		Review Course Syllabus	Johnson
		"Get Acquainted"	Johnson

		Information Processing	Johnson
2	**Jan. 30**	Review Copy Corner Booklet	Johnson
		Enhancing the Lecture	Johnson
		Systematic Instruction Model (see Copy Corner Booklet)	Johnson
3	**Feb. 6**	Cognitive Interaction analysis system (CIAS)	Johnson
		* Paper #1 is due today	
4	**Feb. 13**	CIAS (continued)	Johnson
5	**Feb. 20**	Writing Objectives	_____
		Textbooks	_____
		Getting Started During the First Week	_____
		* Paper #2 is due today	
6	**Feb. 27**	Increasing Student Involvement	_____
		Discussion Techniques	_____
		Motivating Students	_____
7	**March 6**	Cooperative Learning	_____
		Critical Thinking	_____
		Field Studies	_____
		* Paper #3 is due today	
	March 13-17	**SPRING BREAK**	
8	**March 20**	Motivating Students	_____
		Case Studies	_____
9	**March 27**	Simulations and Role-Playing	_____
		Field Trips	_____
		* Paper #4 is due today	
10	**April 3**	Keller Plan and Bloom's Mastery	_____
		Learning	
		Lab Method	_____
		Faculty Evaluation	_____

11	April 10	Term Papers	_____
		Oral Reports	_____
		Faculty Tenure	_____
		* Paper #5 is due today	
12	April 17	Media and Multi Media	_____
		"Hypertext"	David Hutchinson
13	April 24	Testing and Evaluating Student	
		Progress	_____
		* Paper #6 is due today	
14	May 1	**"Pat Brown's In-Basket"Johnson**	
		Complete Formative, Summative Evaluation and Goal Forms	Johnson
15	May 8	**Final Exam Week: no class, but:**	
		* Paper #7 is due by 1:00 p.m. plus any others that haven't been turned in	

BASIC TEXTS AND MATERIALS
(They correlate with the course syllabus, course objectives, and assessment of student outcomes.)

I.   Glenn Ross Johnson (1995). *First Steps to Excellence in College Teaching* (third edition). Madison, WI: Magna Publications.

II. Copy Corner Booklet for EDCI 601 "College Teaching." Copy Corner is located at the corner of Texas Avenue and George Bush Drive in College Station (1710 George Bush Drive; Ph: 693-0640).

III. Wilbert J. McKeachie (1994). *Teaching Tips: Strategies, Research, and Theory for College and University Teachers* (ninth edition). Lexington, MA: D.C. Heath.

Why *First Steps to Excellence in College Teaching*? It is an outgrowth of teaching EDCI 601 "College Teaching." It provides a structure that parallels the topics in the syllabus.

Why the Copy Corner Booklet? It provides documents that support various topics covered during EDCI 601 "College Teaching."

Why *Teaching Tips*? It provides a broader coverage of teaching as an art, and it provides research reports on a variety of topics involved in college teaching.

GRADING

30 points for an in-class presentation (average score of top 50% using form provided in Copy Corner Booklet — see more on this later in the syllabus)

70 points for papers (maximum of 10 points per paper).

Total possible points = 100

Note: Because this course is a highly interactive course and we need your contributions, your grade will be lowered one grade level if you miss three or more class sessions (an "A" will become a "B").

Final grade in course:
90-100 points = A
80-89 Points = B
LESS than 80 points = C

SEVEN REACTION PAPERS

You will type one-page reaction papers to journal articles about college teaching (seven papers). Points will be deducted if you exceed one page per reaction paper. All papers must respond to a current article in a national journal published between Jan. 1, 1993 and the present issue.

The journal articles must be about college teaching (you can't use articles about early childhood, reading, high school biology, elementary or secondary schools).

Papers must be typed, single-spaced, and printed in either 10 pt. or 12 pt. type.

Concentrate on using application, analysis, synthesis, and problem-solving when writing your papers.

Use two subheadings:

Content of the Article

Reactions and Application

Content of the Article (top half of paper; 50% of the paper): Identify the key point (s) made in the article; use quotations and identify the page(s) where the quotations appear in the article.

Reactions and Applications (bottom half of paper; 50% of the paper): Your personal reactions to the article plus an important application statement about how you plan to apply what you learned from the article — how you would use what you learned.

Make THREE photocopies of each paper (keep the original; turn in two copies).

I will grade one of the photocopies and return it; I will retain the second photocopy to deter plagiarism.

Place your pseudonym on the reverse side of the paper. Don't use your real name.

Also, on the reverse side of the paper indicate the number of the paper; e.g., Paper #1.

At the top of the front side of the paper, include the following:

a. author (s) and date of publication

b. title of article

c. name of journal, vol., number, pages

Cross, Patricia K. (1993). On college teaching. *Journal of Engineering Education.* 82 (1) 99-107.

THE FOLLOWING DIRECTIONS ARE IMPORTANT FOR THE SELECTION OF ARTICLES IN NATIONAL JOURNALS:

The **first** article must deal with one of the following topics:

a. writing objectives for a course

b. textbooks

c. the syllabus

The **second** article is one of your choosing, as long as it is about college teaching.

The **third** article must deal with one of the following topics:

a. those first class days OR starting the class OR an article about the first week of classes

b. any one of the categories for the Motivated Strategies for Learning Questionnaire (MSLQ) — see Chapter 3 in *First Steps to Excellence in College Teaching.*

c. audio-tutorial programs (e.g., S. N. Postlethwait's program)

The **fourth** article is one of your choosing, as long as it is about college teaching.

The **fifth** article must deal with one of the following topics:

a. the lecture

b. discussion

c. using the Keller Plan

d. individualizing instruction

The **sixth** article is one of your choosing, as long as it is about college teaching.

The **seventh** article must deal with one of the following topics:

a. case studies in teaching undergraduate courses

b. simulations and/or role playing in teaching undergraduate courses

c. field trips in undergraduate courses

d. teaching labs in undergraduate courses

PRESENTATIONS

Prior to your presentation, provide all students and Dr. J with a copy of your lesson plan plus a copy of the scoring sheet. At the close of your presentation, everyone (including Dr. J) will complete the scoring form for your presentation (the teaching/presentation scoring form is located in the Copy Corner Booklet, and you must complete it and have it duplicated for everyone in the course, including Dr. J.). Dr. J will collect the forms and calculate the average score by using only the highest 50% of the scores plus his score. A score of .5 will be rounded up (e.g., 28.5 will be rounded up to 29) and a score less than .5 will be rounded down (e.g., 28.4 will be rounded down to 28).

GRADES ON PAPERS

Grading of the one-page reaction papers will include the following criteria: sentence structure; proofreading; ability to remain on focus; use of higher cognitive skills in analyzing, synthesizing, and evaluating the article; ability to use application.

Practice Lesson:
Cognitive Interaction Analysis System (CIAS)

Directions: Cover the correct responses in the far right column with a strip of paper. Read each line, identify the category, and record your category numerals on the strip of paper. When you finish, compare your numerals with mine. If they don't match, try to figure why my numerals are different from your numerals. You may want to refer back to the section in this book where I cover the descriptions and ground rules for CIAS.

[Note: put one numeral for each hash mark (/).]

	[beginning]
	0

INSTRUCTOR:

Let's turn our attention now to the topic/	6
of energy./ The need for energy to operate	6 5
machinery, warm our homes, and propel our	
transportation has/ become a critical issue	5
in our country and in/ other parts of the	5
world./ Today we will discuss/ various types of	5 6
energy including nuclear energy./ While	6
discussing this topic in class I want you/	6
to verbally identify at least four sources/	6
of energy. I also want you to verbally/	6
differentiate between fission and fusion/	6
and to identify/ at least one favorable/	6 6
aspect and one unfavorable aspect of/	6
fission and of fusion./ Excluding nuclear	6
energy, what have been our chief sources/	4
of energy?/	4

STUDENT:

Fossil fuels./	8

INSTRUCTOR:

Excellent, Sharon!/ And when we say fossil	2
fuels, what do we have in mind primarily?/	4

STUDENT:

Ah, coal, oil./	8

INSTRUCTOR:

Good, Russ!/ Coal, oil—/can you think of	2 3
another?/	4

STUDENT:

Natural gas./	8

INSTRUCTOR:

Natural gas./ Very good, Lana!/ We do get   3 2
to a certain extent energy from another
source./ Do you know what that source is?   5
Lana?/   4

STUDENT

Water power./   8

INSTRUCTOR:

Water power,/ and in more recent years/   3 5
solar energy has emerged./ So coal, oil,   5
natural gas, and water power have been our/   5
primary sources for energy to the present/   5
with solar energy emerging recently./   5
The increasing demand for fuels,/   5
particularly oil/ by industrialized/   5 5
nations, has created/ a serious problem./   5 5
What is that problem? Lana?/   4

STUDENT:

A diminishing supply./   8

INSTRUCTOR:

Yes, we have a diminishing supply of
fossil fuels./ Many industrialized nations/   3 5
are importing fuel at a great cost. If we/   5
can develop a different source of energy,/   5
particularly if it's cheap and available,/   5
it would be very beneficial to all/   5
countries. One source many are exploring is/   5
nuclear energy. When radioactivity was/   5
discovered near the end of the last century/   5
physicists began to speculate about energy/   5
that might be stored within the atom./ In   5
1911 they realized that the source of the/   4
energy was where?/   4

STUDENT:

In the nucleus./   8

INSTRUCTOR:

The nucleus./Very/good, Sharon!/   3 2 2
Realizing that the energy was in the
nucleus,/ their major problem until 1939   4
was what?/   4

STUDENT:

How to get the energy out of the atom./   8

INSTRUCTOR:

That's it ... how to release the energy in a

useful way./ If we considered the measured/   3 5
masses of atomic nuclei we realize that/   5
there are two ways to make nuclear energy
available./What are those two ways?/ Russ?   5 4 4

STUDENT:

Fission and fusion./   8

INSTRUCTOR:

Fission and fusion./What is fission?/ Lana?   3 4 4

STUDENT:

It's the splitting apart of the atoms./   8

INSTRUCTOR:

Yes, splitting of the heaviest nuclei into
two fairly equal parts./ Well, if that's/   3 4
fission, what's fusion?// Russ?/   4 0 4

STUDENT:

Bringing together of two nuclei./   8

INSTRUCTOR:

The combining of the lighter nuclei./   3
The appeal of fission and fusion will be/   4
what? Lana?/   4

STUDENT:

It's self-sustaining.../it keeps on going.   8 8

INSTRUCTOR:

Very good./ Once started, it has the   2
possibility of becoming/ self-sustaining and   3
producing more energy than/ is consumed and   3
causing the reaction to occur./ When nuclear   3
fission was discovered in 1939, it uncovered/   5
a highly concentrated energy source; and,/   5
we know the history of the development of/   5
the atomic bomb and nuclear reactors. The/   5
availability of uranium is presently/   5
appealing, but fission may not be the/   5
complete solution to the energy problem./   5
Why?/ Russ?/   4 4

STUDENT:

Well, we're running out of uranium, too./   8

INSTRUCTOR:

Eventually we'll probably run into/ a   3
diminishing supply of uranium,/ plus some   3
countries do not have access to uranium./   5
So we now turn to nuclear fusion/ as a   6

possible power source./ What is/ the   6 4
essential fuel material for fusion?/ Lana?/   4 4

STUDENT:

Hydrogen./   8

INSTRUCTOR:

A form of hydrogen./ Do you know what we   3
call that heavy hydrogen?/   4

STUDENT:

Deuterium./   8

INSTRUCTOR:

That's right, deuterium./ Why is this   3
appealing?/ Lana?/   4 4

STUDENT:

Because it's available from water./   8

INSTRUCTOR:

Yes, and we have a lot of water./ It has   3
been theoretically calculated that the/   5
energy potential from the deuterium nuclei/   5
present in a gallon of water is equal to/   5
the combustion of three hundred gallons of/   5
gasoline./ Is it costly to extract deuterium/   5 4
in a gallon of water?/ Russ?/   4 4

STUDENT:

No, it's not./   8

INSTRUCTOR:

No, it's not./ It's cheap, a few pennies/   3 5
per gallon of water./ So the fuel source is   5
cheap, it's abundant,/ it's available.   5
Unfortunately,/ there are several problems/   5 5
about fusion power./ Can nuclear fusion even/   4
be achieved?/ Russ?/   4 4

STUDENT

Yes./   8

INSTRUCTOR:

Yes./ We have been able to do it   3
experimentally./ Laboratories have   5
accelerated deuterium/ nuclei to a high   5
velocity in cyclotrons, and,/ when they hit   5
a solid target containing deuterium,/ fusion   5
reactions take place,/ but most of the   5
energy is dissipated as heat/ in the target   5
because only a small/ number of accelerated   5

deuterium nuclei collide with those on/   5
the target. Thus we spend more energy than
we produce./ It is the search for more ways/   5 6
to generate more energy/ than we spend/   6 6
that we will deal with theoretically during/   6
the next few weeks when we continue our
discussion/ of nuclear fusion./ To summarize,   6 6
we have identified coal,/ oil, natural gas,/and   6 5
water power as our chief sources of energy/   5
with solar energy coming into the picture/   5
in recent years. We differentiated between/   5
fission, the splitting of the heaviest   5
nuclei/ into two equal parts, and fusion,/   5
the combination of the lightest nuclei. The/   5
availability of uranium and the ability to/   5
split the nuclei/ is a strength for fission./   5 5
A limitation is its unavailability to all/   5
nations and eventually a problem with/   5
supply. The appeal of fusion is that it/   5
uses a form of hydrogen, deuterium,/   5
available to everyone in water. The major/   5
limitation is the inability to combine the/   5
lightest nuclei/ without expending more/   5 5
energy than we can produce./ We'll continue   5
with this/ topic next class session./   6 6
[end of transcript]   0

Bibliography

Adams, David L. 1993. Instructional Techniques for Introducing Critical Thinking and Life-Long Learning in Science Courses. *Journal of College Science Teaching* 23 (2): 100-104.

Ahmad, Nazir. 1990. The Use of Video Technology in Education. *Educational Media International* 27 (2) (June): 119-123.

Anastasi, Anne. 1988. *Psychological Testing*. 6th ed. New York: Macmillan.

Ausubel, David P. 1968. *Educational Psychology: A Cognitive View*. New York: Holt, Rinehart, and Winston.

Ball, Samuel, ed. 1977. *Motivation in Education*. New York: Academic Press.

Baren, Robert. 1993. Teaching Writing in Required Undergraduate Engineering Courses: A Materials Course Example. *Journal of Engineering Education* 82 (1) (January): 59ff.

Barratt, Leslie B. 1988. Ten Things That Teachers Should Teach (and Students Should Learn) About Language. *Contemporary Education* 59 (2) (Winter): 70-71.

Beckman, Mary. 1990. Collaborative Learning: Preparation for the Workplace and Democracy? *College Teaching* 38 (4) (Fall): 128-133.

Beegle, John, and David Coffee. 1991. Accounting Instructors' Perceptions of How They Teach Versus How They Were Taught. *Journal of Education for Business* 67 (2) (November/December): 90-94.

Behr, A. L. 1988. Exploring the Lecture Method: An Empirical Study. *Studies in Higher Education* 13 (2): 189-200.

Benjamin, Moshe, Wilbert J. McKeachie, Yi-Guang Lin, and Dorothy P. Holinger. 1981. Test Anxiety: Deficits in Information Processing. *Journal of Educational Psychology* 73 (6): 816-824.

Bennett, William J. 1984. *To Reclaim a Legacy: Report on the Humanities in Higher Education.* Washington DC: National Endowment for the Humanities.

Bergan, John R., and James A. Dunn. 1976. *Psychology and Education: A Science for Instruction.* New York: Wiley.

Berrill, Deborah P. 1991. Exploring Underlying Assumptions: Small Group Work of University Undergraduates. *Educational Review* 43 (2) (February): 143-157.

Berry, J., and T. Graham. 1991. Using Concept Questions in Teaching Mechanics. *International Journal of Mathematical Education* 22 (5) (September): 749-757.

Bishop, M. P. 1992. Computer Issues in Geography: Operating in an Integrated Environment, *Collegiate Microcomputer* 10 (3) (August): 148ff.

Bloom, Benjamin S. 1976. *Human Characteristics and School Learning.* New York: McGraw-Hill.

Bloom, Benjamin S., Max D. Engelhart, Edward J. Furst, W. H. Hill, and David R. Krathwohl, eds. 1956. *Taxonomy of Educational Objectives: The Classification of Educational Goals. Handbook I, Cognitive Domain.* New York: David McKay.

Bloom, Benjamin S., J. Thomas Hastings, and George F. Madaus. 1971. *Handbook on Formative and Summative Evaluation of Student Learning.* New York: McGraw-Hill.

Blum, Albert A. 1991. Education as Emulation. *College Teaching* 39 (2) (Spring): 76-79.

Bok, Derek. 1986a. *Higher Learning.* Cambridge MA: Harvard University Press.

Bok, Derek. 1986b. *President's Report to the Board of Overseers.* Unpublished manuscript. Cambridge: Harvard University.

Borg, Walter R., and Meredith Damien Gall. 1989. *Educational Research.* 5th ed. New York: Longman.

Boud, David. 1992. The Use of Self-Assessment Schedules in Negotiated Learning. *Studies in Higher Education* 17 (2): 185-200.

Boyer, Ernest L. 1987. *College: The Undergraduate Experience in America.* New York: Harper and Row.

Bredehoft, David J. 1991. Cooperative Controversies in the Classroom. *College Teaching* 39 (3) (Summer): 122-125.

Brent, Rebecca, and Richard M. Felder. 1992. Writing Assignments — Pathways to Connections, Clarity, Creativity. *College Teaching* 40 (2) (Spring): 43-47.

Brookfield, Stephen D. 1987. *Developing Critical Thinkers: Challenging Adults to Explore Alternative Ways of Thinking and Acting.* San Francisco: Jossey-Bass.

Brown, George B., and Madeleine Atkins. 1987. *Effective Teaching in Higher Education.* London, New York: Methuen.

Brown, Ian W. 1991. To Learn Is to Teach Is to Create the Final Exam. *College Teaching* 39 (4) (Fall): 150-153.

Brown, James W., and James W. Thornton, Jr. 1971. *College Teaching: A Systematic Approach.* 2nd ed. New York: McGraw-Hill.

Browne, M. Neil, and Stuart M. Keeley. 1985. Achieving Excellence: Advice to New Teachers. *College Teaching* 33 (2) (Spring): 78-83.

Browne, M. Neil, and Stuart M. Keeley. 1988. Do College Students Know How to "Think Critically" When They Graduate? *Research Serving Teaching* (Southwest Missouri State University Center for Teaching and Learning) 1 (9): 1-2.

Browne, M. Neil, and Mary L. Keeley-Vasudeva. 1992. Classroom Controversy as an Antidote for the Sponge Model of Learning. *College Student Journal* 26 (3) (September): 368-373.

Bugelski, B. R. (Bergen Richard). 1971. *The Psychology of Learning Applied to Teaching.* 2nd ed. Indianapolis: Bobbs-Merrill.

Bullard, John R., and Calvin E. Mether. 1984. *Audiovisual Fundamentals: Basic Equipment Operation and Simple Materials Production.* 3rd ed. Dubuque IA: Wm. C. Brown.

Cameron, Beverly J. 1991. Using Tests to Teach. *College Teaching* 39 (4) (Fall): 154-155.

Cameron, L .A., and J. Heywood. 1985. Better Testing: Give Them the Questions First. *College Teaching* 33 (2) (Spring): 76-77.

Camp, William G. et al. 1988. *Microcomputer Applications for Students of Agriculture.* Danville IL: Interstate Printers & Publishers.

Carroll, John B. 1989. The Carroll Model: A 25-Year Retrospective and Prospective View. *Educational Researcher* 18 (1) (January): 26-31.

Chickering, Arthur W., and Zelda F. Gamson. 1987. Seven Principles of Good Practice in Undergraduate Education. *AAHE Bulletin* 39 (7): 3-7.

Christensen, C. Roland, and Abby J. Hansen. 1987. *Teaching the Case Method: Text, Cases, and Readings*. Boston: Harvard Business School.

Clarke, John H. 1987. Building a Lecture That Really Works. *The Education Digest* 53:2 (October): 52-55. Condensed from *College Teaching* 35 (2) (Spring), 56-58.

Colorado, Rafael J. 1988. Computer-Assisted Instruction Research: A Critical Assessment. *Journal of Research on Computing in Education* 20 (3) (Spring): 226-233.

Cross, K. Patricia. 1986. A Proposal to Improve Teaching, or What "Taking Teaching Seriously" Should Mean. *AAHE Bulletin* 39 (1): 9-15.

Cross, K. Patricia, and Thomas A. Angelo. 1988. *Classroom Assessment Techniques: A Handbook for Faculty*. Ann Arbor, MI: National Center for Research to Improve Postsecondary Teaching and Learning.

Cross, K. Patricia, and Thomas A. Angelo. 1993. *Classroom Assessment Techniques: A Handbook for College Teachers*. 2nd ed. San Francisco: Jossey-Bass.

Cross, K. Patricia. 1993. On College Teaching. *Journal of Engineering Education* 82 (1) (January): 99-107.

Dees, Roberta L. 1991. The Role of Cooperative Learning in Increasing Problem-Solving Ability in a College Remedial Course. *Journal for Research in Mathematics Education* 22 (5) (November): 409-421.

Diamond, Nancy A., M. Helgesen, and P. Visek. 1986. *Teaching Large Classes*. Illini Instructor Series, No. 1. Office of Instructional and Management Services. Urbana-Champaign: University of Illinois.

Dohrer, Gary. 1991. Do Teachers' Comments on Students' Papers Help? *College Teaching* 39 (2) (Spring): 48-54.

Downs, Judy R. 1992. Dealing With Hostile and Oppositional Students. *College Teaching* 40 (3) (Summer): 106-108.

Drain, C. B., K. R. Dirks, O. C. Jenkins, J. K. Campbell, K. Finstuen, and Glenn Ross Johnson. 1991. Comparison of Two Instructional Methods on the Levels of Physiologic and Psychologic Stress as Measured by Blood Cortisol and the State-Trait Anxiety Inventory. *Nurse Anesthesia* 2 (4) (December): 172-183.

Duckwall, Julia M., Louise Arnold, and Jeannie Hayes. 1991. Approaches to Learning by Undergraduate Students: A Longitudinal Study. *Research in Higher Education* 32 (1) (February): 1-13.

Duell, Orpha K. 1994. Extended Wait Time and University Student Achievement. *American Educational Research Journal* 31 (2) (Summer): 397ff.

Dunkhase, John A., and John E. Penick. 1990. Problem-Solving in the Real World. *Journal of College Science Teaching* 19 (6) (June): 367-370.

Eble, Kenneth E. 1976. *The Craft of Teaching: A Guide to Mastering the Professor's Art.* San Francisco: Jossey-Bass.

Eison, A., J. Morgan, and P. Marsteller. 1992. Methods for Teaching Investigative Skills in College Introductory Biology: A Pilot to Program. *BioScience* 42 (11): 870-873.

Eison, James. 1990. Confidence in the Classroom: Ten Maxims for New Teachers. *College Teaching* 38 (1) (Winter): 21-25.

Erekson, O. Homer. 1992. Joint Determination of College Student Achievement and Effort: Implications for College Teaching. *Research in Higher Education* 33 (4) (August): 433-446.

Farrow, Margaret. 1993. Knowledge-Engineering Using HyperCard: A Learning Strategy for Tertiary Education. *Journal of Computer-Based Instruction* 20 (1) (Winter): 9ff.

Flanders, Ned A. 1965. *Teacher Influence, Pupil Attitudes, and Achievement.* Cooperative Research Monograph No. 12, U.S. Office of Education. Washington DC: U.S. Government Printing Office.

Flanders, Ned A. 1970. *Analyzing Teaching Behavior.* Reading MA: Addison-Wesley.

Frederick, Peter J. 1986. The Lively Lecture — 8 Variations. *College Teaching* 34 (2) (Spring): 43-50.

Freedman, D. P. 1991. Case Studies and Trade Secrets: Allaying Student Fears in the 'Litcomp' Classroom. *College Literature* 18 (February): 77-83.

Freilich, Mark B. 1989. Frequent Quizzing, the Final Exam, and Learning: Is There a Correlation? *Journal of Chemical Education* 66 (3) (March): 219-223.

Friedlander, Jack, and Peter MacDougall. 1992. Achieving Student Success Through Student Involvement. *Community College Review* 20 (1) (Summer): 20ff.

Fuhrmann, Barbara S., and Anthony F. Grasha. 1983. *A Practical Handbook for College Teachers.* Boston: Little, Brown.

Gadzella, Bernadette M. 1982. Computer-Assisted Instruction on Study Skills. *Journal of Experimental Education* 50 (3) (Spring): 122-126.

Galbraith, Michael W., and Ray E. Sanders. 1987. Relationship Between Perceived Learning Style and Teaching Style of Junior College Educators. *Community/Junior College Quarterly of Research and Practice* 11: 169-177.

Gall, Meredith D., and Joyce P. Gall. 1976. The Discussion Method. In N. L. (Nathaniel Lees) Gage, ed., *The Psychology of Teaching Methods*. Yearbook of the National Society for the Study of Education, Vol. 75, Part I, pp. 166-216. Chicago: University of Chicago Press.

Garland, Daniel J. 1991. Using Controversial Issues to Encourage Active Participation and Critical Thinking in the Classroom. *Community/Junior College Quarterly of Research and Practice* 15: 447-451.

Gayeski, Diane M., ed. 1993. *Multimedia for Learning: Development, Application, Evaluation*. Englewood Cliffs, NJ: Educational Technology Publications.

Geske, Joel. 1992. Overcoming the Drawbacks of the Large Lecture Class. *College Teaching* 40 (4) (Fall): 151-154.

Gleason, Maryellen. 1986a. An Instructor Survival Kit for Use With Large Classes. *AAHE Bulletin* 39 (2) (October): 10-14.

Gleason, Maryellen. 1986b. Better Communication in Large Courses. *College Teaching* 34 (1) (Winter): 20-24.

Glidden, Jock, and Joanne Gainen Kurfiss. 1990. Small Group Discussions in Philosophy 101. *College Teaching* 38 (1) (Winter): 3-8.

Gordon, Steven I., and Richard F. Anderson. 1989. *Microcomputer Applications in City Planning and Management*. New York: Praeger.

Gould, Jeffrey, and Anne Lomax. 1993. The Evolution of Peer Education: Where Do We Go From Here? *Journal of American College Health* 41 (6): 235-240.

Graesser, Arthur C., and Natalie K. Person. 1994. Question Asking During Tutoring. *American Educational Research Journal* 31 (1) (Spring): 104-137.

Grauer, Robert T., and Sugrue, Paul K. 1991. *Microcomputer Applications*. 3rd ed. New York: McGraw-Hill.

Gullette, Margaret Morganroth. 1992. Leading Discussion in a Lecture Course:Some Maxims and an Exhortation. *Change: The Magazine of Higher Learning*. 24 (2) (March/April): 32-39.

Hammons, James O., and Jackson R. Shock. 1994. The Course Syllabus Reexamined. *The Journal of Staff, Program, & Organization Development* 12 (1) (Summer): 5-17.

Hansen, Abby J. 1987. Suggestions for Seminar Participants. In C. Roland Christensen and Abby J. Hansen, *Teaching and the Case Method: Text, Cases, and Readings*, 54-59. Boston: Harvard Business School.

Hawkes, Peter. 1992. Collaborative Learning and American Literature. *College Teaching* 39 (4) (Fall): 140-144.

Heichberger, Robert L. 1991. Quality in College Teaching: The Effective Elements. *College Student Journal* 25 (2) (June): 207-210.

Heinich, Robert, Michael Molenda, and James D. Russell. 1993. *Instructional Media and the New Technologies of Instruction*. 4th ed. New York: Macmillan.

Hess, Carla W. 1988. Thinking About Thinking: Bloom's Taxonomy Rediscovered. *Faculty Development* (Bush Regional Collaboration in Faculty Development) 1 (3): 2-3.

Hollabaugh, Mark. 1989. Textbook Selection: Clearing the Fog. *Journal of College Science Teaching* 18 (5): 327-329.

Hunt, Pearson. 1951. The Case Method of Instruction. *Harvard Educational Review* 21 (3) (Summer): 175-192.

Integrity in the College Curriculum: A Report to the Academic Community. 1985. Washington DC: Association of American Colleges.

Involvement in Learning: Realizing the Potential of American Higher Education. 1984. National Institute of Education, Study Group on the Conditions of Excellence in American Higher Education. Washington DC: U.S. Dept. of Education.

Jackson, Barbara L. 1990. Debating *Huck Finn. College Teaching* 38 (2) (Spring): 63-66.

Jacobsen, Rhonda Hustedt. 1993. What Is Good Testing? Perceptions of College Students. *College Teaching* 41 (4) (Fall): 153-156.

Jennings, Steven A. 1993. Using an Urban "Attractiveness Index" as a Method in Teaching College-Level Field Geography. *Journal of Geography* 92 (1) (January/February): 41-42.

Johnson, Allen B. 1993. Enhancing General Education Science Courses. *College Teaching* 41 (2) (Spring): 55-58.

Johnson, Glenn Ross. 1975. *Improving College Teaching Via Microteaching and Interaction Analysis: A Handbook for Professors and Prospective Instructors*. Abstract ERIC Documents ED 102-933, ED 102-286, 105-067, IR 001-429. Vol. 10.

Johnson, Glenn Ross. 1976a. *Analyzing College Teaching.* Manchaca TX: Sterling Swift Publishing.

Johnson, Glenn Ross. 1976b. Delphi-Process Evaluation of the Effectiveness of Selected In-Service Training Techniques to Improve Community/Junior College Instruction. *Community/Junior College Research Quarterly* 1 (1) (October-December): 51-57.

Johnson, Glenn Ross. 1987a. An Eclectic Systematic Instruction Model for Expository Instruction. *The Journal of Staff, Program, & Organization Development* 5 (3) (Winter): 91-99.

Johnson, Glenn Ross. 1987b. Changing the Verbal Behavior of Teachers. *The Journal of Staff, Program, & Organization Development* 5 (4) (Spring): 155-158.

Johnson, Glenn Ross, Michael O'Connor, and Robert Rossing. 1985. Interactive Two-Way Television: Revisited. *Journal of Educational Technology Systems* 13 (3): 153-158.

Johnson, Glenn Ross, Lynn M. Burlbaw, and Victor L. Willson. 1994. Systematic Instruction vs. Lecture. *The Journal of Staff, Program, & Organization Development* 11 (4) (Spring): 197-201.

Johnson, Glenn Ross, James A. Eison, Robert Abbott, Guy T. Meiss, Kathy Moran, Joyce A. Morgan, Thomas L. Pasternack, Ernest Zaremba, and Wilbert J. McKeachie. 1991. *Teaching Tips for Users of the Motivated Strategies for Learning Questionnaire (MSLQ).* Ann Arbor MI: National Center for Research to Improve Postsecondary Teaching and Learning.

Jonassen, David H., ed. 1988. *Instructional Designs for Microcomputer Courseware.* Hillsdale NJ: L. Erlbaum Associates.

Kagan, Dona M. 1987. Stress in the College and University Classroom: A Synthesis of Eight Empirical Studies. *College Student Journal* 21 (4) (Winter): 312-316.

Kaiser, Barbara. 1988. Cooperative Learning Revisited. *Faculty Development* (Bush Regional Collaboration in Faculty Development) 1 (2): 2-3.

Kamali, Ali. 1991. Writing a Sociological Student Term Paper: Steps and Scheduling. *Teaching Sociology* 19 (4) (October): 506-509.

Karabenick, Stuart A., and John R. Knapp. 1991. Relationship of Academic Help Seeking to the Use of Learning Strategies and Other Instrumental Achievement Behavior in College Students. *Journal of Educational Psychology* 83 (2): 221-230.

Keefe, Thomas J., and John H. Newman. 1994. Using Computers Interactively to Overcome Resistance to Learning About Theory. *The Journal of Staff, Program, & Organization Development* 11 (3) (Winter): 167-179.

Keim, Marybelle C. 1991. Creative Alternatives to the Term Paper. *College Teaching* 39 (3) (Summer): 105-107.

Keller, Clair W. 1993. Using Book Reviews for Cooperative Learning. *College Teaching* 41 (1) (Winter): 26-28.

Kettinger, William J. 1991. Computer Classrooms in Higher Education: An Innovation in Teaching. *Educational Technology* 31 (8) (August): 36-43.

Kiewra, Kenneth A., Nelson F. DuBois, David Christian, Anne McShane, Michelle Meyerhoffer, and David Roskelley. 1991. Note-Taking Functions and Techniques. *Journal of Educational Psychology* 83 (2): 240-245.

King, Alison. 1992. Comparison of Self-Questioning, Summarizing, and Notetaking-Review as Strategies for Learning From Lectures. *American Educational Research Journal* 29 (2) (Summer): 303-323.

Kirby, Susan C. 1987. Self-Evaluation: A Way to Improve Teaching and Learning. *Teaching English in the Two-Year College* 14 (1): 41-44.

Knapp, John R., and Stuart A. Karabenick. 1988. Incidence of Formal and Informal Academic Help-Seeking in Higher Education. *Journal of College Student Development* 29 (3) (May): 223-227.

Korobkin, Debra. 1988. Humor in the Classroom: Considerations and Strategies. *College Teaching* 36 (4) (Fall): 154-158.

Kulik, James A., Chen-Lin C. Kulik, and Peter A. Cohen. 1979. Research on Audio-Tutorial Instruction: A Meta-Analysis of Comparative Studies. *Research in Higher Education* 11 (4): 321-341.

Lacina, Lorna J., and Connie Ledoux Book. 1991. Successful Teaching on Television. *College Teaching* 39 (4) (Fall): 156-159.

Lawrence, Brenda. 1991. Introducing Cooperative Learning in the Classroom. *New Era in Education* 72 (1) (April): 7-14.

Learned, Edmund P. 1987. Reflections of a Case Method Teacher. In C. Roland Christensen and Abby J. Hansen, *Teaching and the Case Method: Text, Cases, and Readings*, 9-15. Boston: Harvard Business School.

Lefrancois, Guy R. 1972. *Psychological Theories and Human Learning: Kongor's Report.* Monterey CA: Brooks/Cole Publishing.

Lidren, Donna M., Steven E. Meier, and Thomas A. Brigham. 1991. The Effects of Minimal and Maximal Peer Tutoring Systems on the Academic

Performance of College Students. *The Psychological Record* 41 (1) (Winter): 69-77.

Locatis, Craig N., and Francis D. Atkinson. 1984. *Media and Technology for Education and Training.* Columbus OH: Charles E. Merrill Publishing.

Lundy, Jane. 1991. Cognitive Learning From Games: Student Approaches to Business Games. *Studies in Higher Education* 16 (2): 179-188.

McKeachie, Wilbert J., *et al.* 1994. *Teaching Tips: Strategies, Research, and Theory for College and University Teachers.* 9th ed. Lexington MA: D.C. Heath.

McLeish, John. 1976. The Lecture Method. In N. L. (Nathaniel Lees) Gage, ed., *The Psychology of Teaching Methods.* Yearbook of the National Society for the Study of Education, Vol. 75, Part I, 252-301. Chicago: University of Chicago Press.

McNamara, James F., and Glenn Ross Johnson. 1980. Verbal Interaction Differences Between Junior/Community Colleges and University Settings. *Community/Junior College Research Quarterly* 4 (June): 277-292.

Mealey, Donna L., and Timothy R. Host. 1992. Coping With Test Anxiety. *College Teaching* 40 (4) (Fall): 147-150.

Michaelsen, Larry K. 1992. Team Learning: A Comprehensive Approach for Harnessing the Power of Small Groups in Higher Education. In Donald H. Wulff and Jody D. Nyquist, eds., *To Improve the Academy* 11: 107-122. Stillwater OK: New Forums Press.

Mickler, M. L., and C. P. Zippert. 1987. Teaching Strategies Based on Learning. *Community/Junior College Quarterly* 11 (1): 33-37.

Miles, Leroy, and Harold W. Stubblefield. 1982. Learning Groups in Training and Education. *Small Group Behavior* 13 (3) (August): 311-320.

Milford, Murray H., S. C. Brubaker, and Glenn Ross Johnson. 1991. Comparison of Systematic Instruction in Soil Science. *Journal of Agronomic Education* 20 (2): 131-135.

Mitch, David. 1990. The Role of the Textbook in Undergraduate Economic History Courses: Indispensable Tool or Superficial Convenience? *Journal of Economic History* 50 (2) (June): 428-431.

Morano, Richard A. 1985. Effective Methods Depend Upon Subject Matter. *College Teaching* 33 (3) (Summer): 134-139.

Morris, Larry W., Mark A. Davis, and Calvin H. Hutchings. 1981. Cognitive and Emotional Components of Anxiety: Literature Review and a Revised Worry-Emotionality Scale. *Journal of Educational Psychology* 73 (4): 541-555.

Murray, John P. 1990. Better Testing for Better Learning. *College Teaching* 38 (4) (Fall): 148-152.

Murray, John P., and Judy I. Murray. 1992. How Do I Lecture Thee? *College Teaching* 40 (3): 109-113.

Naveh-Benjamin, Moshe. 1991. A Comparison of Training Programs Intended for Different Types of Test-Anxious Students: Further Support for an Information-Processing Model. *Journal of Educational Psychology* 83 (1): 134-139.

Newton, Evangeline V. 1991. Developing Metacognitive Awareness: The Response Journal in College Composition. *Journal of Reading* 34 (6) (March): 476-478.

O'Brien, Thomas V. 1991. Test Anxiety in College Students: A Review of the Recent Research and an Endorsement of a Multimodal Approach. *Community/Junior College* 15 (3) (July): 271-282.

Overholser, James C. 1992. Socrates in the Classroom. *College Teaching* 40 (1) (Winter): 14-19.

Parrott, Thena E. 1994. Humor as a Teaching Strategy. *Nurse Educator* 19 (3) (May): 36-38.

Petonito, Gina. 1991. Fostering Peer Learning in the College Classroom. *Teaching Sociology* 19 (4) (October): 498-501.

Pintrich, Paul R., and Glenn Ross Johnson. 1990. Assessing and Improving Students' Learning Strategies. Marilla D. Svinicki, ed. *The Changing Face of College Teaching*, 83-92. San Francisco: Jossey-Bass.

Pintrich, Paul R., Wilbert McKeachie, David A. F. Smith, Robert Doljanac, Yi-Guang Lin, Moshe Naveh-Benjamin, Terence Crooks, and Stuart A. Karabenick. 1988. Motivated Strategies for Learning Questionnaire (MSLQ). Ann Arbor MI: National Center for Research to Improve Postsecondary Teaching and Learning.

Pintrich, Paul R., David A. F. Smith, Teresa Garcia, and Wilbert J. McKeachie. 1991. *A Manual for the Use of the Motivated Strategies for Learning Questionnaire (MSLQ).* Ann Arbor MI: National Center for Research to Improve Postsecondary Teaching and Learning.

Posner, Herbert B., and James A. Markstein. 1994. Cooperative Learning in Introductory Cell and Molecular Biology. *Journal of College Science Teaching* 23 (4) (February): 231-233.

Postlethwait, Samuel N., J. [Joseph] Novak, and H. T. [Hallard Thomas] Murray, Jr. 1969. *The Audio-Tutorial Approach to Learning: Through Independent Study and Integrated Experiences.* 2nd ed. Minneapolis: Burgess.

Powell, J. P., and L. W. Andresen. 1985. Humor and Teaching in Higher Education. *Studies in Higher Education* 10 (1): 79-90.

Powers, Donald E., and Mary K. Enright. 1987. Analytical Reasoning Skills in Graduate Study: Perceptions of Faculty in Six Fields. *Journal of Higher Education* 58 (6) (November/December): 658-682.

Rae, Andrew. 1993. Self-Paced Learning With Video for Undergraduates: A Multimedia Keller Plan. *British Journal of Educational Technology* 24 (1): 43-51.

Ramsden, Paul. 1987. Improving Teaching and Learning in Higher Education: The Case for a Relational Perspective. *Studies in Higher Education* 12 (3): 275-286.

Rewey, Kirsten L., Donald F. Dansereau, and Jennifer L. Peel. 1991. Knowledge Maps and Information Processing Strategies. *Contemporary Educational Psychology* 16 (3) (July): 203-214.

Rieber, Lloyd. 1993. Paraprofessional Assessment of Students' Writing. *College Teaching* 41 (1) (Winter): 15-18.

Rosenshine, Barak. 1976. Classroom Instruction. In N. L. (Nathaniel Lees) Gage, ed., *The Psychology of Teaching Methods.* Yearbook of the National Society for the Study of Education, Vol. 75, Part I, 335-371. Chicago: University of Chicago Press.

Rothkopf, Ernst Z. 1976. Writing to Teach and Reading to Learn: A Perspective on the Psychology of Written Instruction. In N. L. (Nathaniel Lees) Gage, ed., *The Psychology of Teaching Methods.* Yearbook of the National Society for the Study of Education, Vol. 75, Part I, 91-129. Chicago: University of Chicago Press.

Sappington, A. A., and W. E. Farrar. 1982. Brainstorming vs. Critical Judgment in the Generation of Solutions Which Conform to Certain Reality Constraints. *The Journal of Creative Behavior* 16 (1) (First Quarter): 68-73.

Saunders, Danny. 1992. Peer Tutoring in Higher Education. *Studies in Higher Education* 17 (2): 211-218.

Schlenker, Richard M., and Constance M. Perry. 1986. Planning Lectures That Start, Go, and End Somewhere. *Journal of College Science Teaching* 15 (5) (March/April): 440-442.

Schwier, Richard A., and Earl R. Misanchuk. 1993. *Interactive Multimedia Instruction.* Englewood Cliffs NJ: Educational Technology Publications.

Self, Samuel Lee. 1973. Flanders' Interaction Analysis and a Token Economy in College Physics Instruction. Unpublished doctoral dissertation, Texas A & M University, College Station, TX.

Sharps, Matthew J., and Jana L. Price. 1992. Auditory Imagery and Free Recall. *The Journal of General Psychology* 119 (1) (January): 81-87.

Shavelson, Richard J. 1976. Teachers' Decision-Making. In N. L. (Nathaniel Lees) Gage, ed., *The Psychology of Teaching Methods.* Yearbook of the National Society for the Study of Education, Vol. 75, Part I, 372-414. Chicago: University of Chicago Press.

Sheridan, Jean, Ann C. Byrne, and Kathryn Quina. 1989. Collaborative Learning: Notes From the Field. *College Teaching* 37 (2) (Spring): 49-53.

Smith, B. Othanel, ed. 1971. *Research in Teacher Education: A Symposium.* Englewood Cliffs NJ: Prentice-Hall.

Smith, Herman W. 1987. Comparative Evaluation of Three Teaching Methods of Quantitative Techniques: Traditional Lecture, Socratic Dialogue, and PSI Format. *Journal of Experimental Education* 55 (3) (Spring): 149-154.

Smith, Randy J., Diane B. Arnkoff, and Thomas L. Wright. 1990. Test Anxiety and Academic Competence: A Comparison of Alternative Models. *Journal of Counseling Psychology* 37 (3) (July): 313-321.

Snapp, Jim C., and John A. Glover. 1990. Advance Organizers and Study Questions. *Journal of Educational Research* 83 (5) (May/June): 266-271.

Spencer, Donald D., and Susan L. Spencer. 1989. *Drawing With a Microcomputer.* Ormond Beach FL: Camelot Publishing Company.

Stahle, Debra L., and Judith P. Mitchell. 1993. Portfolio Assessment in College Methods Courses: Practicing What We Preach. *Journal of Reading* 36 (7) (April): 538-542.

Starr, Douglas P. 1991. Using Word Processor to Evaluate Student Papers Benefits Student and Instructor. *Collegiate Microcomputer* 9 (1) (February): 55-58.

Sternberg, Robert J. 1985. Teaching Critical Thinking, Part I: Are We Making Critical Mistakes? *Phi Delta Kappan* 67 (3) (November): 194-198.

Symonds, Percival M. 1968. *What Education Has to Learn From Psychology.* 3rd ed. New York: Teachers College Press.

Thiele, Joan E., Joan H. Baldwin, Robert S. Hyde, Beth Sloan, and Gloria A. Strandquist. 1986. An Investigation of Decision Theory: What Are the Effects of Teaching Cue Recognition? *Journal of Nursing Education* 25 (8) (October): 319-324.

Thorndike, Robert Ladd, and Elizabeth P. Hagen. 1977. *Measurement and Evaluation in Psychology and Education.* 4th ed. New York: Wiley.

Tobias, Sheila. 1994. The Contract Alternative: An Experiment in Testing and Assessment in Undergraduate Science. *AAHE Bulletin* 46 (6) (February): 3-6.

Todd, William D. 1982. Brainstorming. *Industrial Education* 71 (2) (February): 22-23.

Tubb, Gary Wayne. 1974. Heuristic Questioning and Problem-Solving Strategies in Mathematics Graduate Teaching Assistants and Their Students. Unpublished doctoral dissertation, Texas A & M University, College Station, TX.

Tyser, Robin W., and William J. Cerbin. 1991. Critical Thinking Exercises for Introductory Biology Courses. *BioScience* 41 (1) (January): 41-46.

Ulsoy, Ali Galip, and Warren R. DeVries. 1989. *Microcomputer Applications in Manufacturing.* New York: Wiley.

Vietor, Donald M., S. C. Brubaker, Murray H. Milford, and Glenn Ross Johnson. 1985. Teacher Improvement Using a Cognitive Interaction Analysis System. *Journal of Agronomic Education* 14 (1): 44-48.

Watson, Jane M. 1986. The Keller Plan, Final Examinations, and Long-Term Retention. *Journal for Research in Mathematics Education* 17 (1) (January): 60-68.

Watson, Scott B. 1992. The Essential Elements of Cooperative Learning. *The American Biology Teacher* 54 (2) (February): 84-86.

Weaver, Richard L., II, and Howard W. Cottrell. 1988. Motivating Students: Stimulating and Sustaining Student Effort. *College Student Journal* 22 (1) (Spring): 22-32.

Weimer, Maryellen. 1987. *Teaching Large Classes Well.* San Francisco: Jossey-Bass.

Weinstein, Claire E., and Douglas Hamman. 1994. Acquiring Expertise in Specific Content Areas: Implications for Teaching Novices. *The Journal of Staff, Program, & Organization Development* 12 (1) (Summer): 57-60.

Wharton, Clifton R., Jr. 1987. Taking Teachers Seriously. *AAHE Bulletin* 39 (9&10): 7-11.

Whipple, William R. 1987. Collaborative Learning: Recognizing It When We See It. *AAHE Bulletin* 40 (2): 3-6.

Williams, David D., Paul F. Cook, Bill Quinn, and Randall P. Jensen. 1985. University Class Size: Is Smaller Better? *Research in Higher Education* 23 (3): 307-318.

Wilson, Jim. 1990. Hypergraphics: "The Classroom of the Future." *THE Journal: Technological Horizons in Education* 17 (7) (March): 65-70.

Wittrock, Merlin C., ed. 1977. *Learning and Instruction.* Berkeley CA: McCutchan Publishing.

Wright, Delivee L. 1987. Selecting the Textbook. *Teaching at UNL.* Lincoln: University of Nebraska-Lincoln.

Wulff, Donald H., and Nyquist, Jody D. 1988. Using Field Methods as an Instructional Tool. In Joanne Gainen Kurfiss *et al.*, eds., *To Improve the Academy: Resources for Student, Faculty, and Institutional Development,* 87-98. Stillwater OK: New Forums Press.

Zeakes, Samuel J. 1989. Case Studies in Biology. *College Teaching* 37 (1) (Winter): 33-35.